THE
APPALACHIAN LEGEND
OF THE
WIZARD CLIP

America's First Poltergeist

MICHAEL KISHBUCHER

FOREWORD BY SCOTT PHILBROOK,
CO-CREATOR OF ASTONISHING LEGENDS PRODUCTIONS

THE
History
PRESS

Published by The History Press
Charleston, SC
www.historypress.com

First published 2023

Manufactured in the United States

ISBN 9781467153812

Library of Congress Control Number: 2023937205

Hi, Dad. Thank you for imparting Barbara Davidson's tale around so many campfires. I used to say that her ghost story fostered a mild obsession, but the term has a new meaning after this project. You left in January, but your grand experiment continues. See you soon.

CONTENTS

Foreword, by Scott Philbrook   7
Acknowledgements   9
Introduction   11

1. The Wizard Clip   17
2. Sources and Main Characters   26
3. Pre-Exorcism Timeline of Events   54
4. The Voice and the Angel   79
5. Religious-Historical Context   90
6. A Legend Forms   105
7. Middleway Today   129

Epilogue: Hauntings, Exorcism, and Mental Illness   137
Notes   143
Bibliography   151
Index   155
About the Author   159

FOREWORD

I've known Mike Kishbucher for a few years and was honored when he invited me to write a foreword for his new book on the Wizard Clip. As a purveyor of folklore and legends in the podcast format for more than eight years, I was surprised when I heard this story from him because it was entirely new to me. On the podcast that my co-host, Forrest Burgess, and I publish, we cover all manner of strange stories. While we've covered some of the more famous ones out there, we also pride ourselves on finding the little-known ones, as they are often the most enticing to research—and our audience certainly enjoys them. So, with all of that lead-in, I'll confess to being taken off-guard at the introduction to such a compelling legend that I knew absolutely nothing about.

As Mike began to give me the broad strokes when he first imparted it to me, I was rapt with attention because, as he and some of his learned colleagues have contributed here, this tale has several hallmarks of a few much more famous stories, such as one we have covered extensively on *Astonishing Legends*, the Bell Witch.

I've been on a fascinating paranormal journey since starting our show in 2014. When we began, I was intent on not only sharing the legends but also looking for proof that something strange had indeed happened in the cases where that applied. Or, conversely, looking for the more mundane explanation behind the legend at hand, because that was just as interesting to me personally as a paranormal smoking gun. But my perspective has significantly changed over the years. I've seen several different flavors of supernatural mysteries and, in researching them, found that many have a great deal of common ground whether they size up to be true or not. The question becomes: why is that ground so common? Is it because of the humanity intertwined with the legends, trying to sort out what's happening and being limited to whatever constructs were available to them at the time? Or is it because there is really some kind of pattern to paranormal interactions? In weighing those questions, I came to a new point of view on it all. It doesn't matter. I stopped trying to convince others that this poltergeist was real or that the mystery was solved. It became more about digging very deeply into the legends themselves and, in doing that, uncovering the true mystery by working past the barrier of trying to convince our listeners that this thing really happened. Nothing ever happens the way it's told later. Trying to prove that it did is futile. So, the disposition I subscribe to now is that the legend is a legend because something definitely happened. The question is what.

There is nearly always the seed of something genuine, unexplained or not, at the root of every legend. It doesn't have to be paranormal, although it might be. As someone who's had an unexplainable personal experience in a haunted house, I have plenty of room for *might*. But what we do now at our show is try to encourage people to get past the probability that the story as told is precisely true. As I said, it doesn't matter. What matters is why the story was told in the first place. Could it have been supernatural, or might it have been something as simple as a political vendetta, as we found in our research on possible origins for the story of the Jersey Devil?

Changing my approach to these tales has allowed me to open my mind to the bigger picture. It's no longer necessary to prove that ghosts are real or that unexplained things occur. Believe that or not, a story like this becomes folklore because something about it resonates with people. The best way to figure out the reality of it is to do the research and focus on what may be implied between the lines. Try to understand the personalities, social pressures, and constructs that dictate the wants and needs of the players involved. There is no one better suited to that task than Mike. He is well equipped to drill down into the minutiae of the fascinating story of the Wizard Clip. His skills and experience as an intelligence analyst offer him tools that I am very envious of. If you want to get to the true bottom of a mystery like this, you'd be foolish to start anywhere else.

SCOTT PHILBROOK,
December 2022

ACKNOWLEDGEMENTS

One of the most critical lessons I've learned in my twenty-five-year intelligence career is the importance of collaborating with proper subject matter experts. I am not a specialist in folklore, history or religion, so early on, I sought the help of several authorities, without whom this project would have never seen the light of day. Heather Moser, an adjunct classics professor at Kent State University and researcher for the Small Town Monsters production company, contributed to sections on Bell Witch lore and European witch hunts and assisted with interviews. Susan Kersey of the Priest Field Pastoral Center invited me for a tour of the grounds and provided incredible insight concerning the history and importance of this legendary location to the Catholic community. Thomas White is a university archivist and curator of special collections in the Gumberg Library at Duquesne University, an adjunct lecturer in Duquesne University's history department, and an adjunct professor of history at La Roche College. Tom is an expert in Ohio Valley folklore, has authored books on Pennsylvania folk magic, and graciously volunteered his valuable time to explain typical late eighteenth-century German American folk beliefs.

Melissa Davies, a clinical psychologist and host of the *Ohio Folklore* podcast, lent her expertise on how mental illness could have affected the formation of the Wizard Clip legend. Pastor Mark Matzke of St. Mark Lutheran Church helped me contextualize the events from a Lutheran perspective. Jon-Erik Gilot, director of archives and records for the Roman Catholic diocese of Wheeling-Charleston, provided valuable source materials for my research.

Middleway walking tour marker. *Author's collection.*

Jessie Norris, president of the Middleway Conservancy, afforded a personal tour of Middleway, relating the legend's vital importance to its residents today. Scott Philbrook and Forrest Burgess of the *Astonishing Legends* podcast encouraged me throughout the process and helped me frame the most useful research questions.

The amazingly talented Lucy Elliot brought an eighteenth-century ghost story to life through her illustrations. Kate Jenkins of The History Press was ever patient and helpful, ensuring that I didn't get off track. Through thorough professional research, Sharon Peery entertained and exhausted my hair-brained genealogical theories. Ted Jackson, Lulen Walker, Christen Runge, and Mary Beth Corrigan of Georgetown University selflessly provided access to source materials virtually from university archives during a time of limited access due to the COVID-19 pandemic. Finally, I must thank my beautiful, tolerant, and ever-reassuring wife, Karrie. Whether I need a sounding board, travel manager, organizer, cheerleader, or simply a smile to lift my spirits, she is always there. I love you, Karrie.

INTRODUCTION

On October 22, 2021, I sat petrified onstage at a Halloween festival in Western Pennsylvania. I started this small event celebrating area folklore with my father in 2019. Due to the COVID-19 pandemic, this was only our second attempt. The first had been an unexpected success, packing so many people into a small outdoor venue that our vendors ran out of food. Instead of chainsaw-wielding clowns and jump scares, we focused that first night on traditional harvest season activities like bobbing for apples and telling regional ghost stories by a bonfire. Full of ourselves, we overshot our mark with the second iteration. It was drizzling and cold, our new venue was too rural, and we foolishly attempted to compete with Friday night high school playoff football.

I was embarrassed, but not because of the paltry crowd. Emboldened by previous success, I invited my favorite podcast hosts to close the evening. Much to my absolute surprise, Scott Philbrook of *Astonishing Legends* accepted my offer and drove more than nine hours to participate. Thinking this would be an excellent opportunity to launch new online content, Scott graciously volunteered his time to host a live YouTube show at our festival. Now he sat opposite me in front of a couple dozen wet, cold, and tired folks. No one else could see us. The internet connection was too weak to broadcast, and I felt sick.

Let's backtrack. In February 2018, I finished writing my first book about legends local to my hometown. Investigating one ghost story, in particular, had become a passion project that spawned this new hobby. It is the first

Pig Lady Festival logo. *Author's collection.*

ghost story I can remember, and I wanted to see if there was any truth behind the folklore that my father and grandfather both loved to retell around backyard campfires. Tennessee has its Bell Witch, and Chicago has Resurrection Mary. We all know Barbara Davidson, the phantom Pig Lady in Beaver County, Pennsylvania. Her tragic story lives on in the small rural community, but beyond that, it is relatively unknown, and I hated to think the legend might fade into obscurity. A few folklorists included the yarn in more extensive regional ghost story compilations, but her tale was never in the spotlight. In 2016, I decided to do something about this and began to gather sources. I felt obligated to ensure that Barbara's account lived on; however, I knew little about storytelling. I was out of my element and turned to podcasts for inspiration. Naturally, I became a fan of *Astonishing Legends*. Scott and Forrest have dived painstakingly deep into folklore origins, facts, and fiction for nearly a decade. This podcast immediately caught my attention. In March 2018, I signed a publishing contract with The History Press for my book *Legends & Lore of Little Beaver Creek*. I also joined in the fun at *Astonishing Legends* as a volunteer researcher that month. I was over the moon.

Fast-forward to late October 2021. Scott, his son, my daughter, and my wife brainstormed show ideas over brunch on the morning of the festival. I was still overly confident that the event would be a success, but he wanted me to take the stage, and I am no showman. Our theme for that year's festival was the famous Portage County UFO chase that had allegedly blown by my hometown in 1966. I was sure he'd want to interview our professional storytellers about that tale. I was wrong, and later that night, I found myself under the lights with Heather Moser discussing the Wizard Clip while trying desperately to hide my stage fright.

I first read this fascinating story while researching the Pig Lady's history. One of the folklore anthologies that includes Barbara's tale, *Devils, Ghosts, and Witches: Occult Folklore of the Upper Ohio Valley*, also briefly discusses the infamous West Virginia story.[1] In a chapter called "Devil's Tales," the Wizard

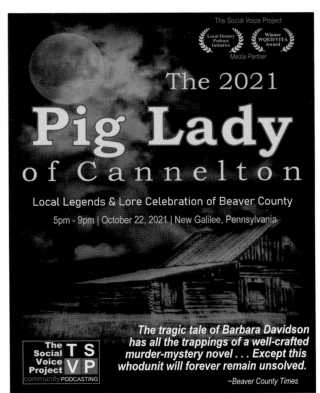

Right: Pig Lady Festival poster. *Author's collection.*

Below: Festival decoration. *Author's collection.*

Clip only occupies a page and a half of the entire book, but its strangeness caught my eye. I've been captivated ever since. It is the story of the United States' first poltergeist and probably its first recorded Catholic exorcism, but few outside the small village of Middleway, West Virginia, know it today. For thirty-five minutes, Scott led us down a rabbit hole of the weird. The conversation convinced me that this legend deserves the same attention I gave Barbara but from a different angle.

Most entertainment media about the supernatural today begins with the premise that claims of hauntings are genuine and that research is only necessary to validate these claims. Much to the chagrin of some, as evident in a few book reviews, I explored each story from a realist perspective in *Legends & Lore of Little Beaver Creek*. As an intelligence analyst, I approach analytic problems using structured techniques to eliminate bias and formulate assessments based on evidence and logical argumentation. So naturally, as a realist, I could not "believe" one way or another about ghost stories because belief is an expression of bias without evidentiary backing.

I explained my intentions to the reader on the first page of the preface. The book's theme is the exploration of local tales with the intent of unearthing either the underlying verifiable roots of each story or possible motivations behind the development of the folklore. Unlike many popular television ghost shows of the past several years, I was not interested in collecting unworldly evidence via electronic voice phenomena recordings or spirit box interaction. However, my research became misguidedly focused on discovering the literal truth. In hindsight, this was a fool's errand. Legends exist as part of history because of what people believed and what they did about it. For example, the results of the Salem Witch Trials are no less horrific or historically significant because our society now rejects the legitimacy of spiritual evidence in court cases.

My research and analysis for that first book revealed that a favorite story from my youth, Gretchen's Lock, is almost certainly a complete fabrication. I hadn't expected a different outcome, but I also didn't begin the effort intending to debunk Gretchen's tale. I love folklore, and my resolve in researching those stories was to renew interest in my hometown's folk legends and preserve them. I nearly excluded my analysis of Gretchen's Lock but ultimately determined the likely motivations behind developing this whimsical bit of folklore justified its inclusion.

This time, I intend to concentrate less on what society considers irrational today and more on understanding the historical context of circumstances that gave rise to those beliefs at that point in history. Societal perceptions of reality are constantly changing due to scientific discovery. Professor Stuart Clark, author of *Thinking with Demons: The Idea of Witchcraft in Early Modern Europe*, best summed up the problem with realist approaches to understanding belief in that they assume that "a mistaken belief cries out for an account of why it continued to be held despite its falseness, other than because it was believed in, while explaining a belief away depends, logically if not actually, on a prior decision that it was incapable of self-support in terms of its reference to something real."[2] In other words, a realist approach to understanding geocentrism would focus on what motivated Aristotle to perpetuate a lie about Earth as the center of the universe rather than why he believed it to be true.

To be clear, I find skepticism valuable and necessary, which is why I find comfort in the realist approach to research. The problem with some professional skeptics of supernatural and paranormal claims is that they can lose their ability to be objective and slip into cynicism. Cynics sanctimoniously portray paranormal claims as irrational, credulous, deceptive, or dangerous. No doubt some purported paranormal witnesses are charlatans, but I have no interest in debunking anyone's story that isn't harmful. Skepticism can be helpful, but cynicism is often a bully's tool.

While thinking about and researching the conflict thesis present in this particular morsel of lore, I frequently found myself experiencing an earworm. The same song repeatedly replayed until I consciously stopped and thought about why it was happening. Then it clicked. One stanza of the song perfectly exemplifies the struggle between faith and reason that I needed to comprehend before beginning the project. No matter how much science reveals about our place in this world, belief in ghosts and the spiritual realm is timeless, culturally ubiquitous, and rational because it provides comfort and optimism that our existence is not finite:

> *We are stardust; we are golden*
> *We are billion-year-old carbon*
> *And we've got to get ourselves*
> *Back to the garden*
> —*Joni Mitchell, "Woodstock"*

I cannot imagine life without fantastic stories. My profession requires me to think about warfare almost constantly, and I find the escapism provided by folklore and contemporary legend therapeutic. For this reason, stories like the Wizard Clip will always captivate my attention.

The Appalachian Legend of the Wizard Clip: America's First Poltergeist is not a ghost story. It is a story about how individuals and groups became motivated to utilize belief in a ghostly legend as a tool for change in the early days of the newly forming American republic. It explores how historical, social, religious, and economic conditions may have influenced the formation of the belief. However, it is not about whether or not the Wizard Clip events were or were not true. For the latter, I agree with Reverend Finotti's assertion in his 1879 monograph about the Wizard Clip: "Oh reader, judge for thyself."

Chapter 1

THE WIZARD CLIP

*There shall not be found among you anyone that maketh his son or his daughter to
pass through the fire, or that useth divination, or an observer of times,
or an enchanter, or a witch. Or a charmer, or a consulter with familiar spirits,
or a wizard, or a necromancer.*
—Deuteronomy 18:10–12

History and folklore are second cousins, related through their mutual
concern with the human record. Many believe something fantastic
happened along Opequon Creek during George Washington's
second presidential term when the tiny Virginia hamlet was called
Smithfield. However, contemporary narratives diverge along two distinct
paths depending on the baseline source materials used when retelling the
account today. Wizard Clip has become a tale of two stories—one history
and another folklore. Both sprang from the same incidences, but the main
story arc is a significant point of disagreement between the two groups most
affected by those events. Wizard Clip is a genuine religious conversion story
to the Catholic community about the miraculous saving of a physically
and spiritually tormented Protestant family. To residents of the village now
called Middleway, West Virginia, the legend places "Clip Town" in the
annals of poltergeist lore alongside Enfield, Amityville, and Pontefract.[3]
We'll begin with a slightly edited version provided by the Middleway
Historical Conservancy, a grass-roots organization dedicated to preserving
Middleway's cultural heritage. Initially published in 1936, this short essay is
by R. Helen Bates.[4]

Neighborhood Wizard Clipp Shop sign. *Author's collection.*

THE LEGEND OF WIZARD CLIP

In the southern part of historical Jefferson County, West Virginia, nestled among the foothills of the Blue Ridge, lies the ancient village of Wizard Clip. The land upon which the village is located was included in the grants made to Mr. William Smith in 1729 by Sir William Gooche, who was the proprietor of that part of Virginia at that time. In 1732, the pioneer home of Mr. Smith was built. Surrounded by majestic hills, this, the first home of Wizard Clip, was placed in a gloomy hollow near a bottomless lake.

Among those that obtained land grants from Mr. Smith was a man named Livingstone. Mr. Livingstone selected land lying along Opequon Creek but also adjoining the village. One night when the sky was inky black, the rain descended in torrents, and the winds rushed through the desolated pines with a wild bellow, a weary Stranger presented himself at Mr. Livingstone's door. With genial hospitality, the traveler was welcomed.

A few hours after retiring, the Stranger sent for Mr. Livingstone and told him he was ill unto death. He requested that a Catholic priest might be sent for at once. Mr. Livingstone was a bigoted man who hated the Catholic Church and swore no priest should enter his house. The Stranger (to whom no name has been given) repeatedly begged that a priest be brought, but his host was obdurate. At the odd hour of midnight, while the elements fought their terrible battle, the soul of the Stranger, unblessed and unshriven, took its flight. The next day his body was buried in unconsecrated ground. For many years his grave was pointed out to the curious.

Then a curse seemed to rest upon Mr. Livingstone and his possessions. A murrain seized his cattle, strange and mysterious sounds were heard about the house, and things were as though ruled by a demon. More dreadful than ought else was clear, distinct, insistent clipping, clipping which went on day and night. The bed linen, family and visitors' clothing, saddles, bridles, and harness were all clipped and always in crescent or half-moon shape. Nothing was sacred from the terrible shears. The witches and wizards were now holding high revels. Mr. Livingstone, pursued by the horror of all this, dreamed a vivid dream in which he saw a man who promised to help him. On Sunday, his wife, a devoted Catholic, persuaded him to go with her to a Catholic service at Shepherdstown. The instant Mr. Livingstone saw the priest, he cried out with streaming eyes, "That is the man who could rid me of the witches." The priest was told the story. The next day he visited the home of Mr. Livingstone at Smithfield (Middleway), sprinkled some holy water on the house's threshold, prayed fervently, and consecrated the ground wherein the Stranger lay buried. He declared deliverance had come. Sure enough, the clipping ceased, "the witches were laid," and Mr. Livingstone was free.

All Souls Chapel, Priest Field Pastoral Center. *Author's collection.*

Moved by gratitude, he gave the Catholic Church forty acres along the Opequon. The Church still owns this land and receives rent from it. It is known as the Priest's Place. For four or five generations, it was in the care of the Minghini family. Recently, however, the Church assumed control. A chapel has been erected on this site, and outdoor meetings are held frequently. It is the ideal spot for camping, and the Church has extended its use as such to all.

The "spell" cast upon the old village of Clip still lingers upon it, and the bottomless lake through which the witches are said to have rushed when the priest exorcised them is still here, and the Opequon flows on, now calmly, now wildly, by the lonely grave of the Stranger.

Next, for comparison, is a 1907 account published in *Woodstock Letters*, a Jesuit periodical issued by Woodstock College from 1872 until 1969, when the school closed its campus in Woodstock, Maryland, near Baltimore. I chose this specific Catholic narrative because it is the first I can find to include a similar stranger or traveler subplot that has become central to the legend. Although this story is over one hundred years old, it has not evolved much since that addition. As with the Bates version, I have lightly edited this from the original for twenty-first-century readability.

The Story of the "Wizard Clip" or "Clip Ghost"
The preternatural manifestations indicated by those names were well known to the Fathers of Maryland, who became priests before the Civil War. In later times they have not been well known, yet they are most interesting. Though they seem like a long and sensational ghost story, they are fully authentic enough for prudent belief, while the narrative is simultaneously truly edifying and instructive.

…They occurred in Jefferson County, at a village called Middleway, since changed, on account of what there took place, to Cliptown, near Martinsburg, [now West] Virginia. Some seven or eight years previously, Mr. Adam Livingston, a Pennsylvanian by birth of Dutch descent, a Lutheran in religion, and an honest, industrious farmer, moved with his family from Pennsylvania to Middleway and soon acquired a handsome property there. He was kind, generous, and hospitable. It was said that a poor Irish traveler, a Catholic, being ill while in Livingston's neighborhood, was taken into his house, carefully nursed and attended through his last sickness, and properly buried. The only thing Mr. Livingston refused to do for the sick man was send for a priest. He had never seen one and

probably held very extraordinary ideas of Catholic priests. Many of his class believed priests were Satan's living emissaries, with horns like their master and other equally enlightened fancies. Therefore, nothing could induce the Livingstons to accede to the dying man's entreaty. This decision came through no hardness of heart, for they were all of kindly disposition, but because to them, the request was absurd, of no consequence, and a great deal better disregarded.

Soon after the death and this refusal, Mr. Livingston appeared to be given over to the buffetings of Satan in good earnest. His barns burned down. All of Livingston's horses and cattle died. Their beds burned. Their clothing and linens were cut into unmendable strips, generally in the form of little crescent shapes. Boots, saddles, and harnesses all shared the same fate. Chunks of fire rolled over the floors without apparent cause; all conceivable noises tormented their ears; their furniture banged about at the most inconvenient times; their crockery dashed to the floor and broken to atoms. These things deprived them of sleep, torturing their nerves and terrifying their very souls, very soon reducing the family to the depths of physical and mental distress. At the same time, they aroused the whole neighborhood to horror and sympathetic advice. Livingston sent far and wide for ministers of all persuasions, for conjurors of all kinds, to come and lay the devil. Still, the evil one gave them the most inhospitable reception, mingled with malice so minute and yet overpowering that it seemed as if he and all his imps were laughing at them. The ministers' tracts and the conjurors' riddles were flung about the house and treated one with as little respect as the other. When it was thought the reverend gentlemen had talked long enough, a great stone apparently kicked down the fireplace, brought their exhortations to a sudden end, and so terrified them that they unceremoniously departed. Less meddlesome visitors were hardly any better treated.

One old Presbyterian lady, says Father Gallitzin, told a company at a tea party that, having heard of the clipping, to satisfy her curiosity, she went to Livingston's house; however, before entering it, she took her new black silk cap off her head, wrapped it up in her silk handkerchief, and put it in her pocket, to save it from being clipped. After a while, she stepped out again to go home; and having drawn the handkerchief out of her pocket and opened it, she found her cap cut into ribbons.

In this hopeless misery, Mr. Livingston was permitted—we may perhaps be allowed to fancy on account of his hospitality to the poor traveler—to have a dream so remarkable and so vivid that it was more like a vision. He dreamed he had toiled up a rugged mountain, climbing it with the greatest difficulty. At the top of the mountain, he saw a beautiful church, and in the church, a man dressed in a style he had never seen before; while he was gazing upon this person, a voice said to him, "This is the man who will bring you relief." He related his dream to his wife and many other persons, one of whom told him that the dress he described worn by the minister of his vision was precisely like that worn by the Catholic priests and advised him to try one of them. But Livingston, discouraged at so many failures, paid little attention to this advice until importuned by his wife, he made inquiries to learn where one could be found. Somebody knew of a Catholic family named McSherry, living near Leetown, where he would be likely to find one. His troubles increasing, his wife entreating, and the conviction forcing itself into his head that a Catholic priest could not work him much eviler than he was already enduring induced him to go to Mr. McSherry's and try. Mrs. McSherry met him at the gate of her residence and asked him his errand; he told her he would like to see the priest, to which she replied that there was no priest there, but one would be at Shepherdstown to say Mass the following Sunday. Mr. Livingston went to Shepherdstown when she told him; the moment the priest, Rev. Dennis Cahill, came out upon the altar to say Mass, Mr. Livingston was so affected that he cried out before the people, "The very man I saw in my dream!" He remained during the service in the most extraordinary agitation and, as soon as the priest returned into the sacristy, followed him, accompanied by Mr. Richard McSherry and an Italian gentleman, Mr. Minghini, who kept a boarding house at Sulphur Springs. These men were among the most prominent of Mr. Cahill's mission and knew somewhat of the circumstances. But no sooner had Mr. Livingston, with tears in his eyes and choking in his throat, made known his errand than the bluff and hearty priest laughed at him and told him his neighbors were teasing him; to go home, to watch them closely, and they would soon get tired of the amusement. The other gentlemen took up his case most earnestly and insisted on the priest's compliance; he reluctantly yielded to them, assured that it was all nonsense, a loss of time, and a very unnecessary journey. When he reached the house and heard and saw pretty clear proofs of Livingston's story, he sprinkled the house with holy water, at which the disturbance ceased for a time. As the priest was leaving, having one foot over the doorsill, a money purse that had disappeared sometime before was laid between his feet.

When Father Gallitzin was there [in 1797], *the disturbances having recommenced, he intended to exorcise the evil spirits for good and all. Still, as he commenced, the rattling and rumbling as of innumerable wagons, with which they filled the house, worked so upon his nerves that he could not command himself sufficiently to read the exorcism, so he was obliged to go for Rev. Mr. Cahill, a man of powerful nerve and hearty faith, who returned with him to Livingston's, and bidding all to kneel down, commanded the evil spirits to leave the house, without doing any injury to anyone there. After a stubborn resistance from the devil, they were finally conquered and compelled to obey the priest. Afterward, Mr. Cahill said Mass there, and there was no more trouble. Father Gallitzin carried a trunk full of clothing that had been cut to pieces during this period of destruction back to Conewago, where they have been seen, even of late years, by eminent priests, who have added their testimony to the truth of these occurrences.*

Scarcely had the Livingston family been relieved from the torments of the devil than they were visited by a consoling voice, which remained with them for seventeen years. It has been supposed that this Voice came from some soul suffering in Purgatory, for some reason, permitted to visit, console, and finally instruct the family. This may have been in return for the hospitality of the poor Catholic who died at their house. In gratitude, perhaps, for the relief he had received at the hands of a Catholic priest and with perfect submission of his will to the truth of the Church, which alone could cast out devils, Mr. Livingston desired, with a portion of his family, to be made a member of it: and after giving them the rudiments of instruction, which were absolutely necessary, Mr. Cahill received them into the Church. Mrs. Livingston complied with this, but she was never sincerely converted.

They had scarcely made their profession of faith and heard one or two Masses before a bright light awoke Mr. Livingston one night, and a clear, sweet voice told him to arise, call his family together, and pray. He did so; the hours passed as a moment, for the Voice prayed with them, leading their prayers. Then it spoke to them, in the most simple yet eloquent manner, of all the great mysteries of the Catholic faith to which they had assented and which, as far as they could, vaguely understanding them, they sincerely and firmly believed. But now, these truths dimly guessed at before and accepted because the Church gave them became clear, intelligible, fascinating, and ever more plain and beautiful. Among other things which they could remember to repeat to others, the Voice said that all the sighs and tears of the whole world were worth nothing in comparison with one Mass, in which a God is offered to a God. It exhorted boundless devotion to the Blessed Virgin Mary, continually imploring them to pray for the suffering souls in Purgatory, whose agony the Voice could never weary of describing, and once, in illustration of their pains, a burning hand was impressed upon some article of clothing directly under the eyes of the family, while it was speaking.

It also urged hospitality and simplicity in dress; it would reprove the least extravagance in which any of them might indulge and induced them to many voluntary penances, long, strict fasts, unbounded charity, and continual prayer. Mr. Livingston, to whom the Voice more particularly addressed itself, was made its agent for innumerable good works. He would be called up at night to undertake long journeys to persons taken suddenly ill or in affliction miles away. He would receive messages without any explanation, which he was enjoined to give at once to different people, to whom they would prove of immense relief, amazing prophecy, and timely warning. It foretold events, which were always verified, and explained the meaning of many others.

Upon one occasion, Mr. Livingston and his family were together in one room when there appeared among them a young man very poorly clad and, though it was a bitterly cold day, barefooted. They asked him where he came from, and he answered: "From my father." Where are you going? "I am going to my father," he said, "and I have come to teach you the way to him." He stayed with them three days and nights, instructing them on all points of Christian doctrine. They asked him if he was not cold, offering him a pair of shoes; he replied that his country was neither hot nor cold. When he left the house, the same idea occurred to each of them: they had not noticed when he came in, so they would watch and see what direction he took when going away. They saw him enter a lot in front of the house and then disappear.

At that time, there was no priest settled in the neighborhood and very few Catholic books to be had even in the large cities, but Bishop Carroll, Mr. Gallitzin, Mr. Brosius, Mr. Cahill, and Father Pellentz and other clergymen, who conversed with Mr. Livingston, were astonished at his knowledge of the Catholic religion and were all convinced that he had been instructed from above.

Fourteen persons were converted in one winter by these things, which were well-known and widely discussed. Others, influenced by the account, received clearer impressions of the reality of another world, of the close proximity of the evil one, and of the intimate union between the Church militant and the Church suffering, from which they were moved to the serious practice of virtue, and to endeavor to live as they wished to die.

...It may be interesting to add that the Voice made a prophecy that remains to be fulfilled. It was that the property in Virginia, left to the Church by Mr. Livingston when he was removed to Pennsylvania in 1820 or sooner, would be a great place for prayer and fasting before the end of time. It was probably the scene of the miraculous manifestations. [5]

Although these short accounts do not include the entirety of the reported events, they represent the essential narrative elements of the story as told by the two cultural groups that claim the legend as heritage. Catholic accounts modulate the pre-exorcism disturbances in favor of emphasizing the later righteous spirit's influence on the family and their neighbors. Secular versions recognize Catholic involvement but accentuate the poltergeist plotline, often ignoring the Voice entirely. I refer to this second grouping of narratives as secular, but not because the authors were irreligious. On the contrary, most were likely Protestant. I refer to these as secular because they are not wholly attributable to one particular denomination as a grouping. Furthermore, religious aspects of the story are not the focus of this set of authors, unlike the Catholic storylines. Next, a more detailed look at the source materials, the story's core personalities, and the timeline of events provides critical details necessary for understanding the belief discrepancies between the two groups.

Chapter 2

SOURCES AND MAIN CHARACTERS

Regarding research, Catholic historians have preserved the most source material regarding Wizard Clip events. The most comprehensive is *The Mystery of the Wizard Clip*, compiled by a priest named Joseph Finotti and published in 1879.[6] Mr. Finotti painstakingly collected available previously written materials, which the McSherry family and Georgetown College mostly held. He then wrote to living witnesses, their children, and knowledgeable clergy, gathering as much additional detail as possible.

More than sixty years later, Raphael Brown's pamphlet, *The Mystery of the Wizard Clip: Diabolical Activity, Priestly Intervention, and Conversions in Colonial America*, was published in 1949 by the Catholic Historical Society in Richmond, Virginia.[7] Part I of the pamphlet is primarily a simplified reorganization of Mr. Finotti's original monograph. Part II describes how the church won back the property, now called Priest Field, from the Minghini family after lengthy litigation in 1922. Brown's most valuable contribution is the inclusion of Adam Livingston's 1802 deed, selling thirty-four acres of his property for one dollar to a trust meant to use the land to sustain the services of a Catholic priest.

Anna Marshall's *Adam Livingston, the Wizard Clip, the Voice*, published in 1978, adds to previous research by including a detailed study of the Livingston family's immigration to the United States and Adam's move from Pennsylvania to Virginia.[8] Finally, the most recent history produced by the Catholic Church is *The Mystery of the Wizard Clip: Supernatural Visitations in Old*

Virginia and Their Remarkable Legacy, authored by the Reverend Monsignor John O'Reilly in 2001.[9] This compilation is essentially a direct reprinting of Raphael Brown's account, with an additional history of the building of the Priest Field Pastoral Center.

These books are well-researched, but as expected, each carries a strong slant toward Catholic principles and dogma. The later histories written in more ecumenical times whitewash some earlier details that could be offensive to Protestants. For instance, they all omitted a passage in Joseph Finotti's original monograph about the Voice describing certain Protestant clergy as "ministers of the devil."[10] Reverend Finotti's version also includes a disconcerting anecdote about the angelic visitor telling the Livingston family, "Luther and Calvin were in hell, and every soul lost to their fault added to their torments."[11]

According to Reverend Finotti, the most authentic remaining document regarding the Wizard Clip events is from 1825, written by Joseph P. Mobberly.[12] Mr. Mobberly was an educated man from Montgomery County, Maryland, and he taught languages at Georgetown College, specializing in English, Latin, and Greek. Mobberly claimed that he copied the story from Reverend Mulledy. According to Mobberly, Reverend Mulledy wrote his version in 1817 at Reverend Anthony Kohlman's request after the two visited Mrs. Anastasia McSherry that August. It is unclear what prompted their visit, but Mr. Mulledy was a native of Virginia and likely knew of the legend. Georgetown University retains Joseph Mobberly's handwritten copy. Mr. Mobberly's short, twenty-four-page document is titled *Livingston's Conversion*.[13]

In his book, Reverend Finotti casually notes that Mr. Mobberly also found work at "St. Inigoes," where he was "in charge of the farm."[14] Mr. Mobberly was likely an overseer of slave labor, from which the diocese benefited for over two hundred years.[15] St. Inigoes was one of several Jesuit-owned plantations from which slave labor funded Society of Jesus (Jesuit) ventures like Georgetown University. The Georgetown University Library system retains the Joseph P. Mobberly SJ Papers, a compilation of Mobberly's writings mainly covering three topics: the Wizard Clip legend, the sacking of Washington, D.C., during the War of 1812, and a multi-part treatise defending the practice of slavery. He died on campus in 1827.

Secular accounts provide less source material but are valuable for describing the haunting. Aside from the story supplied by the Middleway Conservancy, I consulted versions of the Wizard Clip tale collected by folklorists Ruth Ann Musick, George Swetnam, and public historian Joseph Barry. As noted, most

J. Mobberly's hand-painted funeral plaque. *Booth Family Center for Special Collections, Georgetown University.*

Catholic accounts treat the events as authentic, emphasizing the teachings of the Voice and visiting angel. In contrast, secular versions mainly treat the story as folklore, focusing on the poltergeist haunting. It is difficult to determine which accentuating details from either group are embellishments; therefore, I will include the most interesting in the timeline of events chapter that picks up after the Livingston family's move from Pennsylvania.

THE LIVINGSTONS

Although our protagonist and his family left only two primary sources, a property deed and a letter to a newspaper, Catholic historians have collected enough practical detail about the Livingston family to prove their place in the story beyond a shadow of a doubt. Most authors spell Adam's name "Livingston" or "Livingstone." Local public historian Ms. Anna L. Marshall of Kearneysville, West Virginia, provided the most comprehensive historically verifiable record about Adam in her 1978 pamphlet. According to Marshall, Adam Livingston was Pennsylvania Dutch and one of many who moved to the Shenandoah Valley before the Revolution.[16] This resettlement was part of a great western migration, made possible by the Great Wagon Road built in the eighteenth century.

Adam's father, Johann Liebenstein, was a Lutheran who found life under Catholic rule in the German Palatinate[17] intolerable. After decades of Protestant leadership, Johann Wilhelm, a Catholic, became the Elector Palatine in 1690 and invoked *Cujus regio ejus religio* ("whose realm, their religion"). This legal principle meant that the state, which operated the churches, converted to the faith of the state leader.[18] Johann's brother, Charles Philip, succeeded him in 1716, maintaining the oppression of Protestants in the Palatinate. This political change caused a mass migration of Protestants. In 1709 alone, more than thirteen thousand fled the Palatinate for Pennsylvania. By the 1730s, many of these German-speaking families were heading down the Great Wagon Road to America's Appalachian frontier, several of whom harbored strong occult traditions from their recent European experiences. According to West Virginian folklorist Gerald Milnes, this included many born in the Old World who had either experienced or personally known those affected by the Inquisition.[19] In 1851, notable Lutheran pastor and theologian Charles Krauth claimed that witchcraft was so ingrained in local German tradition that he deemed it "impossible to dispel." Pastor Krauth served congregations in Martinsburg and Winchester near Middleway.[20]

When the opportunity to escape religious persecution presented itself in 1732, Johann boarded the ship *Love and Unity* at age nineteen, finally landing in Philadelphia on May 15 after a short stay in Boston.[21] Of the 150 passengers who made the grim twenty-four-week trek from Europe to Martha's Vineyard, fewer than 50 survived the journey. In due time, Johann acquired one hundred acres of farmland in Lancaster County, Pennsylvania, and married Catarina Ruscher on February 12, 1738.[22] The officiating minister was Western Pennsylvania's first circuit-riding

Lutheran pastor.[23] Following the Appalachians, Pastor John Casper Stoever would travel hundreds of miles from northwestern Pennsylvania to Virginia's Shenandoah Valley, preaching in homes and log churches all along the way. This connection may be how Johann later learned about land opportunities in Virginia.

On February 16, 1739, Johann and Catarina's first child, John Adam Liebenstein, was born.[24] Johann and Catarina raised their son in a tightknit German community where he learned the crafts and knowledge his parents and neighbors brought from the old country. His father was a linen weaver, a trade he taught John Adam.[25]

Life was very hard for those living in this part of Pennsylvania from 1745 to 1763. French-allied natives, resenting the western push of British colonial settlers, began raiding the frontier regularly. At the time, the Pennsylvania colony had no militia. British general Edward Braddock's defeat in what is now Western Pennsylvania during the initial stages of the French and Indian War in 1755 worsened the situation, forcing many settlers to move east.[26] The British victory over the French in 1763 did little to stem the attacks, as a confederacy under Chief Pontiac rebelled against the British colonies, mainly in Pennsylvania and in what was then called the Northwest Territory. To retain their lands north and west of the Ohio River, many of these same tribes allied with their former British enemies during the American Revolution. They kept this alliance later during the Northwest Indian War and the War of 1812.[27] Although Lancaster County remained free of raids during the last two conflicts, the threat of attack remained fresh in the minds of all inhabitants. For more than seven decades, life in Penn's Woods was anything but peaceful. Its German residents had escaped the religious wars of their homeland, only to suffer hostility from people they were displacing. For this reason, many of the German and Scotch-Irish immigrants of Lancaster and York Counties looked for safer lands in Virginia.

For better or worse, the Virginia colony was quite different from Pennsylvania. It had a well-organized militia that expelled remaining hostile natives from Virginia's land claims east of the Appalachian Mountains by 1774. Then, on January 16, 1786, the Virginia General Assembly enacted the Virginia Statute for Religious Freedom, effectively separating church and state.[28] This legislation nullified any intolerant laws and practices that lingered from colonial times when the Church of England was the official religious authority of the colony.

Johann purchased a property in what would eventually become Middleway, West Virginia. Unfortunately, Johann died before he could enjoy his new land. In his May 1771 will, Johann stipulated that his son, John Adam, and daughter, Anna Maria, would inherit "all the improvement and tract of land which is situate in Frederick County in the province of Virginia."[29] Jefferson County would later form from this part of Frederick County in 1801. He also gifted John Adam "a weaver's loom and the geers [*sic*] thereunto belonging." This detail is noteworthy later as a potentially presaging factor in Adam's torment by the Clip Ghost.

Johann died two years before the Boston Tea Party on December 18, 1771.[30] Sometime before August 1772, John Adam Liebenstein, now going by the anglicized name Adam Livingston, and his sister, Anna Maria, wife of John Benner, moved their families to the property they inherited in the Virginia colony.[31] Adam's land in what was then called Smithfield totaled 350 acres, and his sister's adjoining plot was 180.[32] Adam's first wife likely died before the move, but Adam's children and at least four enslaved people joined him in the new residence. Adam eventually wed again to a woman named Mary and had more children. The Livingston children included Henry, Eve, George, Mary Ann, Charlotte, Agnes, Jacob, and Catherine.[33]

Interestingly, the 1790 Pennsylvania census lists a man named Adam Livingstone as a head of household in nearby York County, Pennsylvania, and twelve other persons, including four enslaved people, occupied the home.[34] This evidence fits better with the McSherry family tradition, which claims that in early 1790, the Livingstons fled their home in York County, Pennsylvania after mysterious forces began tormenting them. I cannot rule out that two men named Adam with similar surnames lived in the adjoining Pennsylvania counties during the late 1700s, each possessing four enslaved people. Still, the household constructs seem to be a coincidence considering the land and probate records that Ms. Marshall was able to locate.

Nevertheless, the fact that the family held persons in bondage suggests another possible reason for their departure from Pennsylvania if the McSherry tradition is correct. Pennsylvania's Gradual Abolition Act of 1780 prohibited further importation of enslaved people into the state, required Pennsylvania slaveholders to register them annually and established that all children born in Pennsylvania to enslaved people would become free by age twenty-eight regardless of the condition of their parents. Moving to Virginia ensured that the Livingstons could continue the abhorrent practice, including selling off or retaining the children of their servants held in bondage.

THE STRANGER

Mr. Mobberly's 1825 *Livingston's Conversion* does not mention the Stranger, nor does a January 5, 1856 *Catholic Mirror* article titled "The Cliptown Spirit."[35] On August 14, 1885, the *Shepherdstown Register* reprinted an earlier Wizard Clip account from a Winchester newspaper called the *Virginian* from October 1859.[36] This unique version of the story claims that a wealthy German family agreed to give a Catholic priest some property if he would rid their haunted home of "wizards, witches, and devils." However, it does not mention a reason for the disturbance's initiation.

The Stranger appears to be a later character adaptation to fill a problematic hole in the plotline. In this case, the plot error relates to why the Livingston haunting began when it did. It seems that the spontaneity of the haunting didn't sit well with Victorian-era audiences used to tales of vengeful spirits. Hence, storytellers in the mid-1800s began experimenting with two potential plot fixes. The first is a well-worn vengeful ghost trope: crime.

Reverend Finotti's 1879 monograph, *The Mystery of the Wizard Clip*, includes correspondence from John Gillmary Shea explaining how this first plot fix originated.[37] Shea authored the earliest published history of the Catholic Church in the United States and an acclaimed biography of the first American bishop, John Carroll. As he compiled data for these works during the Civil War, he learned that war correspondent James Earl Taylor had embedded with General Sheridan's army, which had encamped not far from Middleway. He wrote to Taylor, imploring him to illustrate the place of the haunting if he could convince a Middleway resident to show Taylor the location. Taylor took on the task of providing sketches for Shea's books. On the back of an illustration of the Livingston property, Taylor wrote:

> *The Livingston, or "Priest's Place" deeded to Fr. Cahill by Mr. Livingston as a penance, is consecrated ground, and the Catholics bring their dead here for burial. The large oaks to the right cover the remains of the dead, and rude stones mark the resting places of those who sleep beneath. There is another burial place in the woods, but I believe it is not on the 35 acres. The people of Smithfield are so superstitious that many will not pass the right of the Field.[38]*

According to Shea, he found out afterward that Mr. Taylor's family had a history with the location, which offered a possible reason for the haunting at Middleway. When these circumstances became known, Reverend Shea asked

James Taylor sketch. *Charles Town Library*.

Mr. Taylor to interview his mother. Mrs. Mary Ann Taylor related that her mother was born in Frederick County, Maryland, in 1782. She asserted that her grandfather, Thomas Poole Esq.; her mother, age ten; and their "black manservant" traveled seventy-five miles from Baltimore on horseback to the "haunted house in Virginia."[39] There they witnessed several strange events, including the inexplicable cutting of clothing left soaped, folded, and laid on a block of wood to be pounded (laundered). Her grandfather claimed that the Livingstons could get no rest:

> *Ministers of all denominations were called in but to no avail. At last, a Catholic priest was called, and the spirit confessed to having murdered his predecessor and that the spirit could not find rest until he had made restitution and given the murdered man a Christian burial. The spirit also made known the spot where the body lay, which was disinterred and witnessed by many residents and strangers. The property was restored to the rightful owner, and the spirit was at rest.[40]*

The inability of a criminal to find rest in death without the aid of living Christians was not a new concept in nineteenth-century ghost stories. The tradition goes back to at least the early Middle Ages with Bishop Germanus's haunted house story. This chronicle is not dated, but Germanus died in 448:

> *One night while the bishop was traveling, his party put up in a ramshackle house, which locals said was haunted. After the Bishop settled in for a night's rest with one of his attendants reading aloud, a dreadful specter appeared before the reader's eyes, which rose up slowly as he watched. All the while, the walls were pelted with a shower of stones. The terrified*

attendant cried out for the protection of the bishop, who awoke and fixed his eyes upon the dreadful apparition. Invoking the name of Christ, the Bishop ordered the spirit to declare who he was and what he wanted. At once, it lost its terrifying demeanor and, speaking low and humble, said that he and a companion were lying unburied after being punished for committing many crimes, which is why they disturb the living. Without proper burial, they could not rest. The ghost led the men to where their bones lay shackled, and the bishop's men dug them up the next day. They dug a grave according to Church law, removed the shackles, recited prayers for the dead, and the haunting ceased.[41]

Hundreds of similar Catholic and Protestant accounts followed, cementing the restless criminal motif as a common reason for hauntings in Christian-dominated countries. Still, this stranger as a murderer variant of the Wizard Clip story is rare. The second fix, a Catholic stranger deprived of last rites by a bigoted Lutheran, likely paired better with earlier versions of the Catholic Wizard Clip narrative. This plot fix is still promulgated by both groups today. The town of Middleway erected a West Virginia Folklife Program "Legends & Lore" roadside sign that features the Stranger narrative prominently, and the custodians of Priest Field maintain a ceremonial Stranger's Grave marker. According to Anna Marshall, the earliest versions of the Stranger's tale didn't appear in print until 1883, in Hardesty's *History of Jefferson County*. Hardesty claims that after moving to Smithfield, Livingston and his family lived peaceably until one fateful evening in 1794, when "a stranger of middle age and respectable appearance made a visit to the place and was received as a boarder" in the Livingston home:

In a few days after the arrival of the traveler, he was taken sick, and as his illness became more threatening, he called Livingston to his bedside, informed him that he was a Catholic, and inquired of him if there was not a priest somewhere in the neighborhood whose services he could procure, should his malady prove fatal, which he had reason to fear it would. Livingston, an intensely bigoted member of the Lutheran church, very gruffly replied that he knew of no priest in the neighborhood and that if there was one, he should never pass the threshold of his door. The dying man repeated his entreaties for the spiritual aid of a Catholic priest, but Livingston was inexorable and refused to countenance his request. The stranger died, his name unknown to his host, and there was nothing among his papers to throw any light upon his history.

The ceremonial Stranger's grave. *Author's collection.*

Livingston employed a man named Jacob Foster to sit up with the corpse on the night of his death. But as soon as the candles were lit in the chamber of the dead, after giving a weak and flickering light, they went out, leaving the room in darkness. They were relighted several times, supposing it to result from some remediable defect in the article, but with the same result. Livingston then brought two candles into the room he had been using in his own family, which were a third burnt down and which he knew to be good. But as soon as they were in the same room with the corpse, they became immediately extinguished. This so alarmed Foster that he abandoned his vigil and left the house. Fifty years ago, the grave of this stranger could be distinctly pointed out.[42]

Reverend Finotti's 1879 monograph almost wholly ignores the stranger plot point except for including a letter written in 1855 by Dr. John McCaffery, president of St. Mary's College.[43] The letter mainly comprises responses to questions posed by John Gilmary Shea, the same historian who uncovered Mrs. Taylor's version that includes a murder as the motive for the haunting. In it, Dr. McCaffery stated, "I do not know where or how I heard that a poor Irish traveler was taken in and nursed kindly by the Livingstons until he died, they refused, however, to send for a priest; sometime after which the clippings began." The Stranger and his grave's location is also a prominent feature of the Wizard Clip plotline in Joseph Barry's *The Strange Story of Harper's Ferry: With Legends of the Surrounding Country* from 1894.[44] As noted in the first chapter,

Stranger's grave marker. *Author's collection.*

Catholic historiographers began adopting the Stranger plot point sometime around 1907, including it in the *Woodstock Letters'* "Clip Ghost" article.

Although the purveyors of Priest Field still recount this version of events today as a cornerstone of the locale's mystique, the dying Stranger portion of the story is unlikely to be rooted in fact. Neither the Mobberly chronicle, the surviving Gallitzin Letters, nor the McSherry family records mention a dying traveler, and most of these accounts suggest that the disturbances began before 1794. Additionally, it is highly suspicious that the family could recall the full name of the man hired to sit vigil with the corpse but never learned the Stranger's name even though he stayed with the Livingstons for "a few days." The dying Stranger appears to be a latter-day embellishment of a small detail provided by Reverend Gallitzin in one of his letters dated April 11, 1839. During his investigation of the events, Father Gallitzin learned that a Catholic traveler boarded with the Livingstons during the disturbances. Gallitzin said nothing about the Stranger dying on the property in the letter and did not mention a murderer:

> *A Roman Catholic peddler who happened to be one night at Livingston's, and who was much disturbed by the noise, which prevailed almost the whole night in the house, tried to persuade Livingston to send for a Roman Catholic priest, but Livingston answered quickly that he had tried so many of those fellows, he was not going to try any more of them.*[45]

Anna Marshall exhaustively studied property records to determine if a previous property owner might have been murdered, with little to show. Furthermore, when the church put the property up for sale in 2020 due to a COVID-19 pandemic–related loss of revenue, the diocese hired a survey company to find and mark the grave sites. Utilizing the latest ground-penetrating RADAR technology, they found no evidence of human burials, including the site currently labeled as the Stranger's Grave, according to Wheeling Diocese archivist Jon-Erik Gilot. If these tombs exist, they are likely on another portion of Adam Livingston's former property.

The McSherry Family

The McSherry brothers, Richard and William, were wealthy Irish immigrants. According to family history, Richard and his twin brother left Ireland for Kingston, Jamaica, at eighteen years old, "where in the course of a few years, they acquired a considerable fortune by their industry and capacity for business."[46] Richard McSherry left Jamaica shortly after the American Revolution. After touring the newly forming nation for some time, he settled in Virginia, where he "purchased large tracts of land in the great valley between the Blue Ridge and Alleghany mountains."[47] He was forty-four when he married eighteen-year-old Anastasia Lilly in July 1791. Richard's family described him as "of fine personal appearance, dressing carefully in the fashion of his day, with lace ruffles, powdered hair, and silver knee buckles."[48] This seemingly nondescript anecdote will become notable later. Despite their age difference, the couple would have nine children.

The McSherrys were an Irish Catholic family living in Virginia at a time when their faith and nationality would have likely made neighbors take notice. At the end of the American Revolution, all but three states retained official religions. By the time of the first Constitutional Convention, five more had legally separated church and state. Regardless, most included checks requiring civil servants to attest to their Protestant religious belief or affiliation to ensure that Catholics could not hold office.[49] Three states—Delaware, Pennsylvania, and Maryland—required only that an officeholder be Christian. With its Virginia Statute for Religious Freedom, written by Thomas Jefferson and enacted in 1786, Virginia was the first to abolish these requirements altogether.[50] Most Catholics born in the British colonies outside Maryland and Pennsylvania had never seen a Catholic church. The McSherrys either traveled to Hagerstown, Maryland, to attend church or hosted services of traveling priests in their home for area Catholics.

John Carroll, the first archbishop in the United States and founder of Georgetown University, became bishop of Baltimore in 1790. At the time, most Catholics in the country resided in Maryland and Pennsylvania. Cecil Calvert, the second Baron of Baltimore, founded Maryland as a refuge for British Catholics in 1634. Quaker William Penn founded Pennsylvania in 1681 as a place of religious freedom and

Bishop John Carroll. *Emmet Collection of Manuscripts Etc. Relating to American History.* Wikimedia Commons, PD-US.

tolerance. In a letter to Cardinal Antonelli, Bishop Carroll described the American Catholic population of 1785:

> There are in Maryland about 15,800 Catholics; all of these are about 9000 freemen, adults over 12 years of age; children under that age about 3000; and about that number of slaves of all ages of African origin called negroes. There are in Pennsylvania about 7000, very few of whom are negroes, and the Catholics are less scattered and live nearer to each other. There are not more than 200 in Virginia who are visited four or five times a year by a priest. Many other Catholics are said to be scattered in other states who are utterly deprived of religious ministry. In the state of New York, I hear that there are at least 1500.[51]

As noted in the account published in the *Woodstock Letters*, the McSherry family lived about four miles from the Livingston farm in a village called Leetown. The McSherrys are essential to the Wizard Clip legend formation for a few reasons. First, Mrs. Anastasia McSherry and some female descendants provided most of the Wizard Clip's primary sources. These include a few surviving letters Anastasia wrote to her brother during the fantastic events and the 1817 interview of Anastasia about the supernatural activity by Catholic priests Mulledy and Kohlman. Father Gallitzin's 1839 letters to Anastasia's daughter Catherine Doll described what he could remember of his time staying with her parents while investigating the strange happenings at the Livingston residence. Finally, one of Anastasia's granddaughters recorded Anastasia's oral history of the fantastic experiences.

Equally notable is the apparent family divide over the authenticity of the events or, at the very least, some male family members' hesitation in validating Mrs. McSherry's claims. We will explore both in the forthcoming chapters. Finally, like many families living in the South before the Civil War, the McSherry name is intrinsically tied to the practice of slavery. The relevance of slavery to the Wizard Clip legend is debatable; however, omitting these facts would be disingenuous to its history. I provide these brief notes, hoping they may give an angle for future scholarship.

The ugly truth is that Adam Livingston possessed enslaved people, and he may have left Pennsylvania to keep profiting from them due to changing attitudes in that state. He then converted to a congregation whose leadership condoned and profited from slavery. Bishop Carroll, whose diocese encompassed all of the United States at the time, owned enslaved people. Many churches in the South participated in the awful

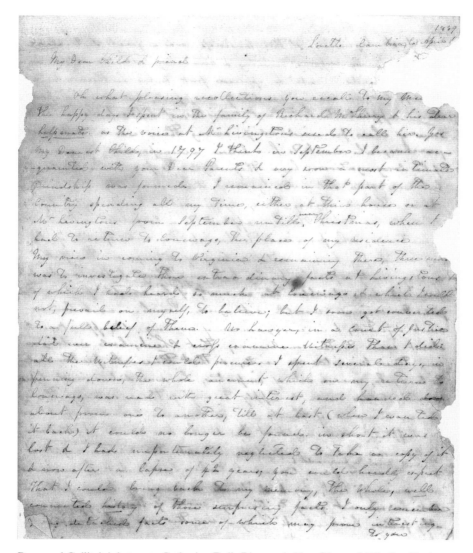

Reverend Gallitzin's letters to Catherine Doll. *Diocesan Archives, Diocese of Wheeling-Charleston.*

practice. Baptist Reverend Richard Furman said in 1823, "The right of holding slaves is clearly established in the holy scriptures, both by precepts and by example."[52] Evangelical Lutheran, Presbyterian, Episcopal, Catholic, and other Christian communities have admitted fault and sought forgiveness and ways to make amends for their role in this dark part of American history.[53]

The McSherry cradle.
Booth Family Center
for Special Collections,
Georgetown University.

A comprehensive oral history chronicled by Mrs. McSherry's granddaughter includes a terrifying anecdote about one of Anastasia's infant sons who allegedly came under demonic attack while resting in a small wooden cradle.[54] This child eventually became a Jesuit priest and rose to the prominent position of president of Georgetown College. Toward the end of his tenure with the school, Reverend William McSherry initiated one of the most notorious single sales of slave labor in U.S. history. In 1838, the Maryland Province Society of Jesus sold 272 enslaved people to Louisiana plantation owners to pay Georgetown College's debt.[55] Georgetown's McSherry Hall was temporarily renamed Remembrance Hall in 2015 due to its namesake's involvement in the sale. The facility was renamed Anne Marie Bancroft Hall after one of the first African American Catholic nuns in 2017. The McSherry cradle is still in possession of the university.

FATHER GALLITZIN, CIRCUIT RIDER, GHOST HUNTER

Reverend Gallitzin's captivating story is the subject of several books. Born into Russian nobility, young Demetrius Augustine Gallitzin could have lived a privileged life but chose to become a Catholic missionary in the United States. His father was Prince Dimitri Alexievich Gallitzin, a Russian ambassador to France and the Netherlands. His mother, the Prussian countess Amalia Von Schmettau, was twenty years younger than his father. As was the custom, the countess converted from her Roman Catholic faith to Russian Orthodox when they wed. However, her husband was not devout. His position caused him to spend much time in Western nations, exposing him to Enlightenment philosophy. Prince Dimitri Alexievich became close friends with Voltaire, Denis Diderot, and Johann Wolfgang von Goethe, all prominent figures of the Age of Enlightenment.[56]

Prince Demetrius Augustine Gallitzin was born at The Hague in 1770. His parents and godmother, Russian empress Catherine the Great, ensured that young Dimitri received the best European education. Catherine ceremoniously commissioned him as a royal officer of the guard at age two, guaranteeing young Dimitri's future was to be gilded. However, by age twenty-four, Amalia had become discontented with her station, and she separated from her much older husband to focus on raising little Dimitri and his sister, Mimi, more modestly. Then in 1786, a severe illness convinced the princess to return to Catholicism. Dimitri also enthusiastically converted at age seventeen, much to his father's disappointment.[57]

At this time, Dimitri's father began planning for his son's future in the military. Usually, male nobility would spend a few years traveling Europe before entering the service. However, the outbreak of the French Revolution made travel unsafe for the aristocracy. Prince Gallitzin intended to send his son to serve in St. Petersburg, hoping that service in the Russian military would lead to his son's return to Russian Orthodoxy. Instead, Amalia used her family's influence to appoint Dimitri aide-de-camp to Austrian general von Lilien in 1792. It did not last long. Following the mysterious sudden death of King Leopold II of Austria and the assassination of King Gustav of Sweden, the Austrian military shed all foreign members.[58]

Because of the unstable European politics caused by the French Revolution, Amalia convinced her estranged husband to allow Dimitri to travel to America. Prussian General von Schmettau, Amalia's brother, proposed that the prince and princess offer Dimitri's service as an aide to President George Washington. Amalia knew that her husband was an admirer of Washington. He agreed, and Amalia secured a priest to escort the young prince abroad. Sometime before his travel, Amalia's priest advised against allowing Washington's religious influence to corrupt her son. Washington was a deist, and Amalia likely decided not to pursue her brother's advice without consulting her husband. She instead arranged for letters of introduction to Bishop Carroll in Baltimore.[59]

For safety, security, and convenience, the prince traveled under Augustine Schmet, later changed to Smith. Arriving in Baltimore in October 1792, "Mr. Smith" quickly became enamored of the bishop and his mission in the newly forming nation. Instead of touring the country, the prince decided

Reverend Gallitzin. *Author's collection.*

Founder of Loretto.
Author's collection.

to forgo his inheritance, enroll in a seminary and become a priest in the United States. Prince Gallitzin was the first priest to conduct all Catholic theological studies in the United States and was ordained on March 18, 1795. His fluency in Russian, French, English, and especially German would become invaluable to Bishop Carroll as he sent the young priest to minister to large immigrant populations in the western part of the country.[60]

Reverend Gallitzin built the first English-speaking Catholic church and congregation west of the Allegheny Mountains, from which he acquired the nickname "Apostle of the Alleghenies." It and the town he founded, Loretto, eventually grew to more than ten thousand members.[61] His mission covered vast swaths of Western Pennsylvania, Maryland, and Virginia, requiring traveling hundreds of miles routinely to attend to his parishioners' needs.

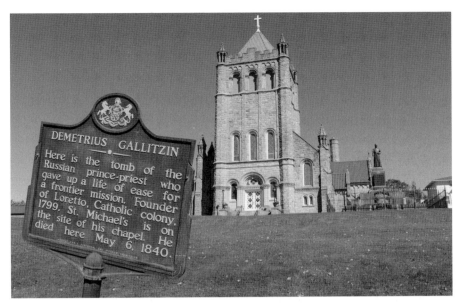

Reverend Gallitzin's Pennsylvania historical marker. *Author's collection.*

Reverend Gallitzin's tomb. *Author's collection.*

Reverend Gallitzin's language abilities may be why the diocese sent him to assist an Irish priest in investigating disturbances at a German Lutheran home in Smithfield, Virginia.

It is hard to understand why almost all accounts of the Wizard Clip outside the Catholic histories exclude his participation—particularly considering that two letters he wrote to the McSherry family in 1839 include firsthand details of the events. The earliest surviving Catholic account of the incidents, copied by Joseph Mobberly in 1825, only mentions Reverend Smith (Gallitzin) twice.[62] Near the end, Mr. Mobberly lists "authorities," or witnesses, as proof that the events were authentic. The authorities section records Reverend Smith agreeing with Dr. Carroll's (Bishop Carroll) claim that Adam Livingston likely received divine instruction, implying that it was from the Voice. The only reference to Smith or Cahill outside of the "authorities" postscript is a brief anecdote toward the end in which the Voice instructs Mr. Livingston to seek out a priest for the sickly Mrs. Minghini. The Voice informs Livingston that he would meet both priests, "but Mr. Smith was the one intended for the woman, as being of a milder nature."

It is curious why this early account spends so little time confirming Gallitzin or Cahill's involvement if they performed the exorcism, especially considering this version is allegedly the result of an interview with Mrs. McSherry in 1817. Reverend Cahill moved back to Ireland in 1806, but Reverend Gallitzin was still accessible in Loretto, Pennsylvania. Adam Livingston had also left Middleway by 1817 but was not far away in Bedford, Pennsylvania, where he died in 1820.[63] Several of Adam's children also lived in either Bedford or Loretto, but it appears that Reverend Kohlman and Mulledy did not interview these witnesses. Regardless, Demetrius Gallitzin faithfully served the community he built until he died in 1840. In 2005, the Vatican officially named the prince priest a Servant of God, the first step toward canonizing a saint.[64]

THE PHENOMENA: A HEX OR HAUNTING?

The destructive entity and Voice as characters reveal much about the particular group telling the Wizard Clip story. An obvious point of divergence between the secular and Catholic narratives is the inclusion of the mysterious Voice. In a later chapter, we will explore the Voice more deeply as it correlates to Catholic views of Purgatory. However, as a lead into the next chapter, which presents a timeline of events, a discussion about the destructive phenomena as it relates to the historical context of late eighteenth-century America is essential.

As evident in the competing Wizard Clip story examples provided in the previous chapter, narratives written by Protestant authors tend to attribute the destructive activity to witchcraft. In contrast, Catholic authors ascribe the violent affair to evil spirits or ghosts. The name Wizard Clip suggests that the Livingstons and probably their Protestant neighbors initially blamed sorcery for the preternatural attacks on the Lutheran family.

Belief in ghosts, witches, necromancy, and exorcism is ageless, and the ability to interact with the deceased is a near-universal concept in ancient cultures. The Babylonian Code of Hammurabi, written sometime between 1755 and 1750 BC, references a water test for examining witches similar to later European ducking techniques. Khonsuemheb and the Ghost, an Egyptian story thought to be from the 20th Dynasty (1189–1077 BC), explains how a high priest of Amun pacifies a wrestles spirit. Thucydides, the ancient Greek historian, described how the Spartan general Pausanias was haunted nightly by a noblewoman from Byzantium that he unintentionally murdered. The First Book of Samuel describes how Saul sought out the Witch of Endor to summon Samuel's spirit for his advice in battling the Philistines. The author of that story may have borrowed from an earlier Roman account. According to the poet Lucan, a Thessalian witch named Erichtho summoned a spirit from the underworld to reveal the outcome of a future battle for the Roman General Sextus Pompey. Lucan also describes how Erichtho uses body parts stolen from graves and infants' blood in her necromancy. Later, the notion of revenants, defined as apparitions of souls in Purgatory requiring human intervention to find eternal peace, developed during the High Middle Ages.[65]

This belief in Purgatory matured within the Catholic Church but likely has much older roots. The Ancient Greeks believed in a place between Elysium and Tartarus called Asphodel Fields, where the souls of those who were neither pure enough to enter paradise nor deserved damnation resided. Rabbinic Judaism teaches that unworthy souls spend up to one year in the fires of Gehenna for spiritual purification. Once cleansed, the worthy would move on to paradise, whereas the wicked would receive additional torture and eventual destruction.[66]

The belief in Purgatory and the sale of indulgences, ostensibly to reduce the amount of time spent there, led Martin Luther to challenge papal authority with his Ninety-Five Theses in 1517, sparking the Protestant Reformation. Martin Luther could not find scriptural backing

Saul and the Witch of Endor. *Gustave Doré, Wikimedia Commons, PD-US.*

for the notion of Purgatory and saw the church profiting by the sale of indulgences as an abuse of power. Calvinist ideologies took hold in the English-speaking world soon after, seeking to further reform the Church of England from its remaining Catholic precepts. Congregationalist, Evangelical Anglican, Reformed Baptist, and Presbyterian denominations emerged from this movement.[67]

Portrait of Martin Luther. *Lucas Cranach the Elder, Wikimedia Commons, PD-US.*

Chief among the reformist ideas of the time is the Protestant doctrine of the cessation of miracles.[68] Reformers contended that miracles were only necessary as divine proof that Christian principles were righteous over pagan beliefs during apostolic times and were unnecessary after the formation of the true church. It provided an argument that Catholic supernaturalism was substantiation that their concepts were false. Therefore, the belief that apparitions are souls permitted to return from Purgatory was deceitful. To reformers like Louis Lavatar, souls immediately departed for Heaven or Hell after death, and praying for them or purchasing indulgences to reduce their suffering in Purgatory was meaningless. Louis wrote in his 1570 book *De Spectris*, "As for those that have been conned into throwing away good money on the souls of the dead; they have been falsely taught by monkish frauds or illusions of devils or their own frantic imaginations or frivolous and vain ideas."[69] He argued that any true spirits are not men's souls but angels or demons, mostly the latter. He claimed that the Catholic Church espoused purgatorial beliefs because of its financial value and utility as a tool of social control.

Regardless of the doctrine of the cessation of miracles, unusual events continued to capture the attention of reformed congregations in the seventeenth and eighteenth centuries, leading to the renewed use of a medieval-era classification of activity between the supernatural, meaning something performed by God and the natural. Preternatural events consisted of unusual occurrences that depended on secondary causes outside God's ordinary province.[70] Therefore, to Reformed Protestants, an apparition resulted from necromancy performed by a witch imbued with power through a pact with the devil.[71]

Under British rule, Puritanical principles influenced the governance of northern American colonies outside of Quaker Pennsylvania. Southern colonies were mainly Anglican (Church of England), other than the Catholic minority in Maryland. Protestant Britain constantly warred with rival Catholic European colonial powers, Spain and France, throughout the colonial period.[72] Until Britain's 1763 victory over France in the French and Indian War, Britain's North American colonies were surrounded on three sides by Catholic powers. Anti-Catholic attitudes persisted until France and Spain sided with the American rebellion, ensuring American success in the Revolutionary War. While Anti-Catholic attitudes lingered in the burgeoning nation, a new class of politicians heavily influenced by the Enlightenment and weary of European religious discord sought ways to enshrine religious tolerance as a fundamental human right.

American views on the preternatural were at an inflection point in 1790. Just under one hundred years had passed since Puritan Congregationalists executed nineteen people and a dog[73] in Salem, Massachusetts, for witchcraft. Another five died in prison, and an eighty-one-year-old man succumbed to torture as his accusers attempted to extract a plea. Those accused were said to have conjured spectral forms to pinch, poke, strike, choke, and generally terrify some of the village's adolescent girls—activity that, on its own, looks pretty similar to other poltergeist cases. However, because it was occurring in puritanical Salem, the doctrine of the cessation of miracles dictated that sorcery had to be the cause. This concept was not new to the English-speaking world. Necromancy was assumed to be the blame for several seventeenth- and eighteenth-century poltergeist-like incidences in Britain, such as the Drummer of Tedworth, the Devil of Glenluce, and the Stockwell Ghost. Belief in conjuring or necromancy likely influenced later Bell Witch folklore development in Tennessee, as the entity causing that poltergeist activity declared itself "Kate Batts' Witch" in 1817. Kate Batts was a neighbor of the protagonist in that story, which we will discuss more in a later chapter.[74]

Witchcraft accusations in the colonies continued but never again achieved the level of the fervor of Salem as Enlightenment ideals of reason and tolerance took hold. By 1790, the American Enlightenment was at its zenith. Many of the U.S. founding fathers were deists, Christians who rejected the notion of divine revelation in favor of practical reason and the observation of nature as evidence for the existence of God.[75] However, Enlightened thinking could not eliminate spiritual belief from the American population entirely. The Second Great Awakening began that year, which further

Witchcraft at Salem Village. *William A. Crafts,* Pioneers in the Settlement of America: From Florida in 1510 to California in 1849, *Wikimedia Commons, PD-US.*

evolved Protestant views on the supernatural by its end around 1840.[76] Nevertheless, the new political climate of 1790 posed a unique opportunity when Catholic supernaturalism and Protestant occult beliefs could coexist in late eighteenth-century Appalachia.

Popular fiction of the early nineteenth century reflected this variance in belief. American Enlightenment ideals certainly influenced Washington Irving's 1820 short story "The Legend of Sleepy Hollow," where Ichabod Crane's credulity and superstition about the supernatural are central themes. However, by 1843, Charles Dickens's immensely popular novella *A Christmas Carol* featured the tormented ghost Jacob Marley. Marley is allowed to return to haunt the protagonist, Ebenezer Scrooge, as a warning to change his ways. This and Marley's bearing of heavy chains as a punishment for his wickedness in life are reminiscent of older Catholic Purgatory tales. The term *poltergeist* did not appear until the penning of *The Nightside of Nature* in 1848, the same year that the Fox family of Hydesville, New York, became afflicted by poltergeist activity that eventually gave rise to Spiritualism.[77] Kate and Maggie Fox experienced some accusations of witchcraft for their communing with the dead, but by then, American society had mainly moved on from demonizing women in this manner. What was once considered necromancy had become evening parlor room entertainment.

Conversely, Catholic belief in the supernatural and Purgatory was largely unmoved in 1790 and remains steadfast today. In the foreword of Raphael Brown's 1949 pamphlet on the Wizard Clip, he carefully described three classes of demonic physical attacks one might suffer from, as understood by the Catholic Church: infestation, obsession, and possession. Citing Father Walter Farrell, Brown's book describes infestation as consisting "of an attack centered on the surroundings of a man rather than himself; noisemaking, throwing things about, breaking articles of furniture, mysterious knocks on doors, and so on." Essentially, this form of spiritual assault is commonly known as poltergeist activity.[78]

The second form, obsession, is a personal attack–inducing physical injury to instill terror. Father Farrell stated that obsession "does not go beyond the attack that any man might make on another by blows or kicks." Finally, the worst kind of attack is possession. The identification of two factors determines possession, according to Brown. First is the devil's presence in the possessed body and the devil's dominion over that body. Three principal signs identify possession: speaking an unknown tongue or understanding it when spoken by another, making known distant and hidden things, and exhibiting a strength out of proportion with one's age and circumstances. An exorcism can remedy all three forms of spiritual attack.[79]

Although the term *poltergeist* didn't arise until the mid-nineteenth century, Raphael Brown pointed out that in 426, Augustine of Hippo (St. Augustine) penned an account in his work *The City of God* that describes an infestation. Interestingly, like the Catholic telling of the Wizard Clip legend, the location of Augustine's exorcism also became a place of worship and miracles afterward:

Hesperius, of a tribunitian family and a neighbor of our own, has a farm called Zubedi in the Fussalian district, and, finding that his family, his cattle, and his servants were suffering from the malice of evil spirits, he asked our presbyters, during my absence, that one of them would go with him and banish the spirits by his prayers. One went, offered there the sacrifice of the body of Christ, praying with all his might that that vexation might cease. It did cease forthwith, through God's mercy. Now he had received from a friend of his own some holy earth brought from Jerusalem, where Christ, having been buried, rose again on the third day. This earth he had hung up in his bedroom to preserve himself from harm. But when his house was purged of that demoniacal invasion, he began to consider what should be done with the earth, for his reverence for it made him unwilling to have it any longer in his bedroom. It so happened that I and Maximinus, Bishop of Synita, and then my colleague was in the neighborhood. Hesperius asked us to visit him, and we did so. When he had related all the circumstances, he begged that the earth might be buried somewhere and that the spot should be made a place of prayer where Christians might assemble for the worship of God. We made no objection: it was done as he desired. There was in that neighborhood a young countryman who was paralytic, who, when he heard of this, begged his parents to take him without delay to that holy place. When he had been brought there, he prayed and forthwith went away on his own feet, perfectly cured.[80]

Chapter 3

PRE-EXORCISM TIMELINE
OF EVENTS

Thou shalt not suffer a witch to live.
—Exodus 22:18

As noted earlier, Adam Livingston almost certainly moved his family from Pennsylvania to Smithfield around 1772, when he was in his thirties. Anastasia McSherry's descendants later claimed that the move happened in 1790 following the initiation of disturbances in Pennsylvania that followed the family to Virginia.[81] This claim contradicts the land records acquired by Anna Marshall, and it conflicts with the earliest written Catholic history of Wizard Clip events available, which states that the Livingstons moved "about the year 1770."[82] The reported primary source of this account is an 1817 interview with Anastasia McSherry, suggesting that the McSherry account changed over time.

Destructive Disturbances Begin

Almost all accounts claim that the Livingston family suffered from the poltergeist for years before seeking help from the Catholic Church. According to Anna Marshall, the haunting began sometime before 1791.[83] She based this date on the earliest surviving written account of the hauntings by Georgetown College language instructor and Jesuit plantation overseer Joseph Mobberly. Mr. Mobberly claimed, "When I was a boy of 10 to 12 years of age, I remember to have heard much talk of the Wizard Clip, a name given to the place by the vulgar…. I lived about 30 miles from the place."[84] Mr. Mobberly was born in 1779, suggesting that Smithfield had acquired the nickname Wizard Clip by 1791. A letter from Reverend Lawrence Slyvanus Phelan, a priest from Hagerstown, Maryland, published in the *Potomak Guardian* on August 29, 1798, claims, "Few there are in Martinsburg or Winchester but have heard of Livingston's ghosts and revelations. These seven or eight years past."[85] As previously mentioned, Mrs. Mary Ann Taylor stated that her mother was born in 1782, and she witnessed some of the destructive events at age ten.[86] Regardless of multiple sources pointing to an earlier start date, most contemporary accounts claim that the haunting began in 1794 when the mysterious Stranger passed away without receiving the last rites. From here, it is challenging to determine the order of events concerning the poltergeist. Modern Catholic and secular versions now recognize the Stranger's death as the haunting's impetus regardless of its uncertain history, so let us pick up where we left off in the Hardesty narrative:

> On the night succeeding the Stranger's burial, the peace of Livingston was much disturbed by the apparent sound of horses galloping around his house. He frequently rose during the night—a beautiful moonlight night—to satisfy his mind, and while he could distinctly hear the tramp of steeds, he could see nothing to assure him that it was anything more than a figment of his imagination.[87]

Most sources claim that fire began erupting from the fireplace the following night for no apparent reason. It happened on several occasions throughout the early evening. The adults and older children burned themselves, corralling red hot coals and blazing logs, ultimately choosing to extinguish the flames and suffer from the cold rather than risk the home burning. Many frosty restless nights followed as the activity seemed to grow in intensity. Loud knocks on the doors and bangs on the walls occurred at all hours, with no visitor found. More worrisome, their beds spontaneously burst into flames on several occasions, requiring quick action to save the home.[88]

The Livingstons could not find rest during the day either. Furniture would bang into the home's walls on its own, and the Livingstons' dishes and crockery indiscriminately flew off of shelves and from cupboards, shattering on the floor and terrifying the children. After several days of intense activity within the home, a very peculiar anomaly started to occur outdoors. The Livingston farm ran alongside a major commercial thoroughfare. Teamsters began complaining about a sturdy rope (that only they could see) tied between trees on the opposite sides of the road, blocking their travel. This scene repeated for several weeks, with each passing wagoner harshly castigating the poor Livingstons.[89]

Valuables began to go missing. Adam's money disappeared from his safe. On another occasion, Rosa McSherry and Eve Livingston were bleaching a new piece of linen and had stretched it out on the lawn to dry. Because of its length, forty yards, this cloth was costly. It disappeared in front of them and was missing for three weeks. After many prayers, the girls found the linen neatly folded and bleached on a bush.[90]

About one month into the haunting, the entity began a new method of torment from which the legend gets the name Wizard Clip. This aspect of the haunting allegedly persisted for years, eventually earning the village the nickname "Cliptown." In my opinion, public historian Joseph Barry best illustrated the events:

> *Over time, the demon, now acknowledged to be around the place, adopted a new method of annoyance. The family began hearing the clipping of invisible shears around the house as the entity cut crescent shapes into their clothes, tablecloths, and bedcoverings. Of course, the news of these unearthly doings soon spread, and people from all directions crowded to see and hear what was happening. Visitors' handkerchiefs, folded in the pockets of their owners, were cut in this peculiar way by the demon of the scissors that kept up his "clip-clip" around them while they were condoling with the affected family.*
>
> *On one gruesome afternoon, a lady visitor was complimenting Mrs. Livingstone on a fine flock of ducks waddling through her yard on their way, perhaps, to the neighboring Opequon Creek when "clip-clip" went the uncanny and invisible shears. One after another, the ducks were cleanly decapitated in broad daylight before the very eyes of the ladies and many other witnesses.*
>
> *One night a party of youngsters of both sexes assembled at the house for a frolic, got up by the young men of the neighborhood, who desired to show to the world and especially to their sweethearts that they were not afraid. Curiosity led many young ladies to the scene, despite the terrors of the place. They were, perhaps, desirous of testing the courage of their lovers and trusted for protection to the big crowd in attendance. One rough, blustering fellow came from Winchester, carrying his rifle. He was courting a girl from the neighborhood of Livingstone's place and determined to show off to the best possible advantage. Things proceeded smoothly for a while, and the*

"Clipped Dress." *Lucy Elliot.*

young people were engaged in a dance when, suddenly, "clip clip" went the goblin shears, and the Winchester hero felt something flap against the calves of his legs. He reached down to investigate and found, to his consternation, that the most important part of his nether garment had been cut loose from the waistband and that there was nothing left for him to do but to sit down and keep on sitting until the festivities were over. His condition soon became known to the others, and, great as the terrors of the situation were, nothing could prevent the company from snickering. Eventually, the hapless hero found his plight so painful that he resolved to leave the house, which he was obliged to do delicately by backing to the door while the ladies coyly looked in another direction.

On another occasion, the neighborhood tailor began boasting that he would spend the night at the haunted house and expose the imposter. Before doing so, he needed to deliver a new broad-cloth suit he finished making that day for one of the Livingston's neighbors. As he passed the haunted farm, "clip clip" went the invisible shears near the ears of the tailor, who, in a plentitude of incredulity, invited the entity to "go for damn." He proceeded to his customer's home and opened his bundle with confidence to exhibit the suit, when lo and behold, he found the clothes full of crescent-shaped slits and utterly ruined.[91]

Other authors would expand Mr. Barry's anecdote about the decapitated ducks, claiming that the Livingstons could not keep other fowl, such as chickens or geese, as the Wizard would destroy them similarly. Another well-used plotline is of the silk cap. Reverend Gallitzin first revealed the account of the "old Presbyterian lady" and her clipped silk cap in a letter he wrote to Mrs. McSherry's daughter in 1839.[92] Gallitzin never mentions the character's name in the letter. Mr. Littleton from nearby Charlestown identifies her as Dorothy McClure in retelling the account for the *Wheeling Daily Intelligencer* in 1891:

Old Dorothy McClure, whom a good many people here remember, declared to the end of her life that she once suffered in this way. She said she called out of curiosity and that just before she entered the house, she took off her best cap and put it in her pocket to protect it. She stayed ten minutes, and when she left and felt for her cap, she drew it out in a dozen pieces.[93]

In researching the Wizard Clip, I initially assumed that the unique clipping part of the haunting had something to do with Adam's father's profession.

Johann Liebenstein was a linen weaver; he taught Adam this trade and left Adam a weaver's loom in his will. I could not substantiate any ties between the clipping as a particular irritant and Adam's weaving skillset other than its resemblance to an older folktale, the Devil of Glenluce.[94] Regardless, this strange element of the story is most well known, and a few groups allegedly kept evidence of the clipping for a time. Joseph Mobberly claimed to have seen some of the clipped clothing in 1813, left by Adam Livingston at a church in Conewago, Pennsylvania, several years before:

> *When I went to New York in 1812, I was directed to call on Father Grassi, who was then at the Sulphur Springs in Virginia, in the neighborhood of Smithfield or Wizard Clip. Mr. McGinny,[95] who then kept the Springs, accidentally mentioned Livingston to us in the course of conversation and observed that Livingston's history was a very strange and curious one and that though he never before had given credit to anything of the sort, yet he knew not how to disbelieve the Clip history.*
>
> *When I was in Conewago in 1813, I saw some clothes deposited by Mr. Livingston or one of his sons. They were cut in several places, and I think I saw I.H.S. on one of the pieces.[96] The Rev. Mr. De Barth told me that there had been a shirt or a towel that had the print of a man's hand*

"I.H.S." example in Loretto, Pennsylvania. *Author's collection.*

burnt into it, but it was then lost or misplaced. I asked him if it appeared to be burnt. He said it seemed as if someone had rubbed his hand on the bottom of an iron pot and then pressed his hand upon the cloth, having the entire appearance of a man's hand.[97]

More information about that last curious detail will follow shortly. Mr. Mobberly further asserted that Mr. Joseph Minghini said Adam Livingston first came to him looking for a priest, but he laughed at him, saying that someone was playing a prank. Only then did Mr. Livingston go to Mrs. McSherry for help. Mr. Minghini also claimed to have gone to the Livingston home and saw cut items lying on the floor. He claimed that he picked up pieces of clothing from the floor cut curiously with the thread as if a tailor had done it. He noted that the cutting was not going on in his presence, as it had ceased sometime before.[98]

Dr. Jedediah Huntington said in his December 1855 *St. Louis Leader* newspaper article, "A few circumstances are imprinted deeply on our memory. One of these was the existence (at Conewago, we think) at a recent date, of some physical evidence of the reality of the clipping and other phenomena, at the house of Mr. Livingston. Including a boot that seemed whole but descended in a long spiral strip when lifted by the top."[99] Regrettably, these remnants of the Wizard Clip haunting did not endure. In an 1872 letter to Reverend Finotti, a Jesuit missionary named J. Enders asserted that the clipping evidence left by Adam Livingston at Conewago remained until 1830 when Father Lekeu had it burned. Mr. Enders provided no reason for the destruction of the items.[100]

All accounts agree that the Livingston family suffered the depredations of the haunting for numerous years, yet interestingly, many describe them as an annoyance. Perhaps the frequency of activity reduced, or the family became accustomed to and unafraid of it until one fateful night when the fires returned. Adam's barn burned to the ground, and all his livestock perished. As a farmer, this was the last straw. Adam began to look for spiritual help.

THE MINISTERS

Both Catholic and secular adaptations claim that Adam Livingston initially requested assistance from several Protestant ministers. According to Reverend Gallitzin's 1839 letter to Anastasia McSherry's daughter, Mr. Livingston first sought the help of his Lutheran pastor:

The good old man reading in his Bible that Christ had given to his minister power over evil spirits, started from home to Winchester, Virginia, and having tears in his eyes, related to his minister (Parson S----t) the history of his distress, losses, and sufferings, begged him to come to his house and exercise in his favor the power he had received from Jesus Christ. The parson candidly confessed that he had no such power. The good old man insisted that he must have that power, for he found it in his bible. The pastor replied that the power existed only in old times but was done away with now. The old man, although living in this "Enlightened Age," had not sagacity enough to understand the distinction between old times and new times, but according to your minister's rule, believed nothing but what he contained in the bible. He, therefore, concluded that parson S----t could not be a minister of Christ, and having left him, he applied to other persons calling themselves ministers of Christ, some of whom promised relief.[101]

According to Anna Marshall, the Lutheran minister in Winchester from 1785 to 1812 was Christian Streit. Pastor Streit was chaplain of the 3rd Virginia Regiment during the Revolutionary War and was taken prisoner in 1780 by the British in South Carolina and held until an exchange of prisoners in 1782.[102] This detail resonated with me as a veteran. Pastor

Reverend Streit's grave. *Author's collection.*

Streit likely suffered horribly under King George III, who refused to provide captured rebels prisoner-of-war status. Instead, he ordered their detainment as traitors in large concentration camps in New York City, Philadelphia, and Charleston, South Carolina. The unlucky were kept offshore below decks in appalling conditions on sixteen prisoner ships with low supplies and rampant disease. More than ten thousand died.

Christian was licensed to minister by the Synod of Pennsylvania in 1769. In 1785, a year before the Virginia Statute for Religious Freedom passed, Pastor Streit became the first Lutheran minister in Winchester, Virginia. According to his diary, he preached throughout the Shenandoah Valley in German and English to the early settlers along the valley pike, which was part of the Great Wagon Road. Realizing that the source materials gathered for this study almost exclusively express nineteenth-century Catholic perspectives, I asked Heather Moser to interview Pastor Mark Matzke of St. Mark Lutheran Church about the state of the Lutheran Church during Adam Livingston's time. They further discussed the relationship between Catholics and Lutherans in the 1790s and Lutheran thoughts on ghosts and witchcraft at the time. Here is a transcript of his thoughts on the matter:

The church hardly had a foothold in the U.S. in the 1790s. Primarily German-speaking Lutheran immigrants were coming through, and in many cases, they were just trying to survive. Much of the clergy immigrating were fleeing nations where there was no separation between church and state, and they were either being suppressed from practicing their religion or were being told what they could or could not preach. It was almost a religious refugee situation. Some were leaving established state-run and funded churches, which meant the pastor was an employee of the state. For reasons of conscience, they left all of that behind. They were starting new lives in the New World, and from a congregational and financial perspective, they were starting from scratch, which was tenuous at best.

The historical relationship between The Lutheran and Catholic Church in America in the 1790s was contentious. I would describe it as not complimentary and bitter due to the Reformation's history, and it was culturally acceptable back then to paint each other in the worst possible terms. To the degree that some Lutherans probably taught that Roman Catholics and their rituals are not Christian. It is much more amicable today. Hymns written by Luther are now sung in Catholic churches. The two organizations work together on common externals like feeding people experiencing homelessness. Certainly, it's true that there are still folks harboring old prejudices on both sides, but in the modern setting, there has been a successful movement toward "live and let live."

At this time in history, there was still a supernatural understanding of witchcraft, ghosts, et cetera, which means that there is a clear line between good and evil and that any fascination with witchcraft or consulting the dead would undoubtedly be framed as something to be avoided. Especially among the early Dutch and the German Lutheran churches in the colonies, there would have been a relatively orthodox understanding of the supernatural being real, as the Bible inescapably talks about supernatural causation for all sorts of things. It describes that there are realms that we typically cannot see or sense that impact our lives. I would presume that the people, and particularly the pastor involved with this, would have taken it seriously, mainly because, at the time, there would have been a grave worry about losing members of the congregation to other groups, in particular, the Catholic Church because of the Reformation history.

However, interestingly, western European thought began to change in the 1700s and 1800s, which certainly bled over into Lutheran Christianity, and many protestant churches in general, creating the idea of the historical-critical method of interpreting scripture. Meaning that we are progressing as human beings, and science is changing our thinking. So, we must look at anything miraculous in scripture with a jaundiced eye and try to explain as much of it away as we can in naturalistic terms. The reference to "old times" in Reverend Gallitzin's letter suggests that the Enlightenment and historical-critical methodologies influenced Adam Livingston's Lutheran pastor.[103]

The viewpoint of the Lutheran pastor in this scenario probably was that there were other causes for the Wizard Clip disturbances, such as mental illness or deception. This approach would likely be less appealing to the Livingston family because the Catholic identification of a demonic attack offers a more concrete answer to their obvious trouble. My seminary professors would say, "That's part of the problem." When you demythologize your religious faith, it creates a challenge when tending to the needs of someone who believes they are dealing with a spiritual problem.

For whatever reason, Adam was dissatisfied with Pastor Streit's level of support, so he next sought assistance from Episcopalians. Ms. Marshall's research indicates that Mr. Livingston likely sought help from the impressive Episcopalian minister Reverend Alexander Balmain.[104] She describes Reverend Balmain, a Scottish immigrant, as having led an esteemed life. The

Pastor Mark Matzke. *Provided by Mark Matzke.*

Christ Protestant Episcopal Church, Winchester, Virginia. *Author's collection.*

influential Lee family hired him to tutor Richard Henry Lee (grandfather of Robert E. Lee). Richard Henry Lee would later become a Virginia delegate to the Continental Congress, where he proposed the first motion to declare independence from Great Britain. He served a one-year term as the Continental Congress president and as a U.S. senator for Virginia from 1789 until he died in 1792 at age sixty-two.

After tutoring the Lee children, Reverend Balmain also became a chaplain in the Revolutionary army and married a close relative of President James Madison. They were settled in Winchester when the Livingston troubles began. At the time, Reverend Balmain ministered at Christ Protestant Episcopal Church in Winchester. Reverend Balmain was likely the first clergyman to investigate the haunting. He probably believed that the family was under spiritual attack, as according to Dr. Jedediah Huntington, Reverend Balmain attempted the first exorcism, but it didn't go well.[105] Balmain was abused by the scornful spirit "so that the prayer book he used was found subsequently in one of the rooms, in a place which indicated no great respect for 'our admirable liturgy' on the part of the ghost." Dr. Huntington implies that the book found its way into a chamber pot. Interestingly, before converting to Catholicism in 1849, Dr. Huntington was an ordained minister of the Episcopal Church.[106]

Adam didn't stop seeking help after the first failed exorcism. Next to offer service was an unnamed Methodist minister and some of his congregation. They may have been from Middleway, but I could not confirm it. The group visited the house and, according to the letter written by Father Gallitzin, "began to pray and bawl, but were soon silenced and driven away by a shower of stones thrown among them by invisible hands."[107]

Joseph Mobberly identified the next group of three men to attempt to rid the house of its spiritual troubles as coming from Winchester but did not reveal their religious affiliation. Perhaps Adam Livingston had finally convinced Lutheran brethren from his church in Winchester to try to assist. The source only tells us that "as soon as they entered the house, a large stone was seen to proceed from the fireplace and whirl upon on the floor upwards of 15 minutes without any stone being missed, upon which the gentleman instantly sneaked away."[108] Assuming that the three men from Winchester were from Adam's Lutheran Church, I asked Pastor Mark Matzke to describe Lutheran thinking about exorcisms:

I have whole books of services for different situations like weddings and funerals, but there is no formal Lutheran exorcism procedural or even a

"A Shower of Stones." *Lucy Elliot.*

Ruins of Adam Livingston's Lutheran Church in Winchester. *Author's collection.*

euphemism for it. The closest thing is "A Brief Service for the Blessing of a Home." In this case, there are a few references to scriptural verses that discuss darkness and light but nothing that approaches the language of exorcism. It would be up to the Lutheran pastor, armed with their knowledge of scripture, to go to relevant passages and use those in sort of a declaration to Satan or his forces that he is marshaled to leave.

Today, if a family were experiencing a demonic presence affecting their lives, a Lutheran pastor would be apt to enter carefully into that situation and exhaust all other potential reasons, such as mental illness. Having done that, a Lutheran would then use the word of God and prayers in God's name with the understanding that Christ is ultimately the exorcist. This situation is nothing to be treated lightly, but one does not have to be trained in a certain way or use a particular rite or ritual to be effective. If you go into a situation like this believing faithfully and using the word of God, then evil will be compelled to leave. I have been in a handful of infestation situations using Catholic terminology, and I've gone to those places and essentially said prayers and read scripture. In those cases, this effort was enough for a tangible change in the feel of those homes.

To Lutherans, there are no clear-cut benchmarks for identifying demonic attacks. The pastor in that situation today would be in consultation with some elected support people to collectively determine the wisest course of action. If other potential causal factors, such as mental illness, are ruled out, then they would enter into more of a direct scriptural confrontation.

FOLK MAGIC PRACTITIONERS

Father Gallitzin wrote in a letter that "after trying ministers in vain, old Mr. L. applied to a conjurer in the South Mountain, who promised to banish the evil spirit if Livingston would pay him a certain sum of money on the spot. L. wisely refused to pay him beforehand but promised to pay double if he would perform the job. The conjurer would not agree. Poor Mr. L. went home dejected in consequence of so many disappointments."[109]

Joseph Mobberly's account of the conjuror differs slightly. It states, "He applied to three conjurors who gave some herbs, a book, and a riddle to catch the Devil, but the first night, the book and herbs were put into a chamber pot and covered with the riddle. The book was the Church of England prayer book."[110] Whether or not Dr. Huntington conflated the chamber pot detail from Mobberly's version with Reverend Balmain's story is unknown. Regardless, Adam's discontinuation from seeking the assistance of recognized Protestant clergy in favor of conjurers suggests that he sought help fighting a witch. This factor may be why the legend's name Wizard Clip endures rather than Clip Ghost. Enlightenment era Protestant clergy would be less likely to entertain these ideas, but Adam was becoming desperate. The reference to conjurors likely means folk magic practitioners, which would have been customary among the German communities of the time. I interviewed Thomas White, author of *Witches of Pennsylvania: Occult History and Lore*, about why Adam may have sought their help. Here is what he had to say:

> *Adam would have been exposed to the practice of Pennsylvania German (or Pennsylvania Dutch) folk magic, commonly known as powwow. The belief in powwow was widespread and could be practiced by anyone, though certain people were more adept at the craft. Powwow was one side of a belief system encompassing healing, protection, and what we would call good magic. On the other side were witchcraft and hexing. Witches were believed to get power from the Devil and committed supernatural harm to the community. However, it is essential to note that both Protestants and Catholics would practice folk magic. The most famous book of charms used*

Thomas White. *Provided by Thomas White.*

by the Pennsylvania Germans, The Long Lost Friend, *was written by a Catholic German immigrant named John George Hohman.*

The majority of the U.S. population in the 1700s still carried at least some belief in folk magic and the supernatural. Disturbances perceived as supernatural could be attributed to witchcraft, demons, or ghosts, depending on the circumstance. The belief that a witch could hex someone was common, and such disturbances were often attributed to witches. There are similar cases in Pennsylvania and Tennessee. Though today we would quickly label the incident as a poltergeist, witches were believed to be able to invisibly harass people, attack them in their sleep, change into animals like cats and wolves, and cause other disturbances.

Prayer books and Bibles were used regularly by folk magic practitioners to invoke the protection and help of God. Many folk magic charms, such as those used by German Brauchers[111] or powwowers, directly invoked Jesus, God, and the Holy Spirit. In the Livingston case, the herbs and the riddle were almost certainly components of a folk magic charm meant to rid the house of the hex and protect against the witch or evil spirit. Folk magic practitioners of all types used ritualized objects in addition to spoken elements and gestures.

Being raised in Lancaster as a Protestant, it makes sense that Adam would turn to a folk healer before a priest. There are numerous charms to protect against witchcraft and evil, which were employed regularly by many German-speaking people then. Protective charms were commonly used inside many homes and barns. It was widely believed that witchcraft could be reversed, and witches could be exposed through various means, including making a witch bottle.[112] *There were even methods for supernaturally killing a witch from a distance if necessary.*

Though many folk magic practitioners worked for free to provide healing, protection, and the location of missing persons, items, and animals, some were thought to be particularly good at dealing with witches and evil, who would sometimes charge fees. These people were known as Witch Masters or Hex Doctors, though there were other names. The South Mountain conjurer mentioned by Reverend Gallitzin was likely one of these.

Catholic Intervention

In most versions of the legend, after much suffering, Adam Livingston eventually has a dream in which he sees a man dressed in unfamiliar robes, and a voice tells him, "This is the man who will bring you relief." After this, his wife convinced Adam to seek a Catholic priest. However, this explanation differs from the recollection of one of the original investigators. Father Gallitzin wrote in a letter to Mrs. Catherine Doll, a daughter of Mr. McSherry, "Your worthy father was the one who overcame Livingston's obstinacy, so far as to permit him to bring a priest to his house. With a good deal of ado, Mr. McSherry prevailed upon the Reverend Dennis Cahill to attend the Livingstons."[113] This small anecdote is interesting in and of itself, not only because Father Gallitzin doesn't mention Adam's prophetic dream but also because Mr. Richard McSherry later allegedly distanced himself from acknowledging the haunting altogether.

Initially skeptical, Father Cahill's first visit to the Livingston farmhouse accounted for nothing more than a home blessing accompanied by the sprinkling of holy water. However, Father Gallitzin reported that a sum of money that had gone missing from Mr. Livingston's chest appeared at the door sill as the priest crossed its threshold. After this, the home became quiet for several days, according to Gallitzin.[114]

The terrifying events returned in earnest within a week, and the family contacted Father Cahill again. Researchers have yet to locate a written account of what Reverend Cahill did next; however, he likely wrote to his superiors requesting advice. At this time, the center of Reverend Cahill's mission was Hagerstown, Maryland, where he erected a log house and chapel. He was one of the missionaries who came directly under the authority of Reverend James Pellentz, Bishop Carroll's vicar for Pennsylvania, western Maryland, and northwestern Virginia (now West Virginia).[115] Father Pellentz resided at a missionary center in Conewago, Pennsylvania, more than ninety miles from Hagerstown. Also living at the mission center was the young Reverend Smith (Gallitzin), whom Father Pellentz likely sent to investigate the situation and assist Reverend Cahill. In the same letter written to Mrs. Doll, Reverend Gallitzin states:

> *I remained in that part of the country, spending all my time either in their home* [her parents, the McSherrys'] *or at Livingston's from September until near Christmas* [1797] *when I was to return to Conewago, then my place of residence. My view in coming to Virginia, and remaining there three months, was to investigate those extraordinary facts at Livingston's, of which I had heard so much at Conewago and which I could not prevail myself to believe, but I was soon converted to a full belief of them. No lawyer in a court of justice did ever examine or cross-examine witnesses more strictly than I did of all those I could procure.*[116]

Then and today, the authority to approve the rite of exorcism lies with the presiding bishop. Only Bishop Carroll could direct such activities and almost certainly ordered a thorough investigation first. Gallitzin would have been a good choice for this assignment, especially if the Livingston family mainly spoke German, as was suggested in several accounts. First, he was one of a few priests in the region not yet assigned a parish. Also, his German heritage and fluent language capability facilitated the investigation by improving communication and putting the Livingstons at ease. Father Cahill likely did not understand German and, being from Dublin, probably spoke English with a heavy Irish accent.

No known comprehensive record of the Middleway exorcism is available to the public. Father Gallitzin claimed to have written a complete account of the Wizard Clip events but lent it out to members of his congregation, and it became lost. He undoubtedly provided a copy to Bishop Carroll, but it is unknown if the church still retains it. Sarah Brownstone mentioned the exorcism in her biography *Life of Demetrius Augustine Gallitzin: Prince and Priest*. For the book, she interviewed Reverend Bradley, who claimed to be a close acquaintance of Reverend Gallitzin and served as Gallitzin's assistant during the last ten years of his life. Ms. Brownstone wrote:

> *When Father Gallitzin was there, the disturbances having recommenced, he intended, as he related afterward to Rev. Mr. Bradley, to exorcise the evil spirits for good and all, but as he commenced, the rattling and rumbling*

as of innumerable wagons, with which they filled the house, worked so upon his nerves that he could not command himself sufficiently to read the exorcism so that he was obliged to go for Rev. Mr. Cahill, a man of powerful nerve and hearty faith, who returned with him to Livingston's and bidding all kneel down commanded the evil spirits to leave the house without doing any injury to anyone there. After a stubborn resistance on the part of the devil, they were finally conquered and compelled to obey the priest. Afterward, Mr. Cahill said Mass there, and there was no more trouble.[117]

Without Father Gallitzin's report, there isn't much information about the events beyond hearsay. It is also difficult to date the exorcism, although if Reverend Bradley is correct, it would have happened in the fall of 1797. Reverend Gallitzin never mentioned his exorcism participation in his existing written accounts. However, he claimed to have copies of Anastasia McSherry's letters, including "interesting facts and advice communicated by Livingston to your mother at the command of the Voice," written, "I think in November 1796 or 1797."[118] If the Voice appeared after the exorcism, it happened before she wrote the letters.

Reverend Gallitzin monument, Loretto, Pennsylvania. *Author's collection.*

I credit Ms. Marshall with finding the most compelling evidence not provided by folklore and church histories. In a letter to the editor published by the Shepardstown-based newspaper, the *Potomak Guardian*, on September 12, 1798, Mrs. Livingston corroborated that strange happenings were still occurring and alluded to another potential reason for the family's difficulties.[119] One potentially implicates the Catholic Church in stoking her husband's superstitions to swindle him of the property:

> *Ask Mr. Phelan why he said the Bishop sent him to visit Livingston's family in this troubled situation and now states in his piece that "it was mere curiosity" that brought him from his business in Martinsburg "to the little town called Wizard Clip."*
>
> *For my part, whatever the spent might have said, whether true or false, I believe it to be one well instructed in the pernicious doctrines of the Romish tenants. I now take the liberty of stating to the public that the trouble still remains in Livingston's family, at times to a greater or less degree, despite Priestly art. Whatever it is, it is wonderful and unaccountable to the most penetrating mind. But what is most unhappy for me, it, aided by Priestcraft, has been the means of secluding me from the business of my family, the embraces of an affectionate husband, and fixed me as an object of public contempt. However, it is finally thought if Priests and Spirits could frighten me to relinquish my claim to my lawful thirds of Adam Livingston's estate, the public ear would be no longer thus amused, but this I leave for time to prove.*
>
> *Mary Ann Livingston*
> *Smithfield, September 12th, '98*

This letter appeared in the local newspaper one year after Reverend Gallitzin began his inquiry. It seems that for Mary, the exorcism had not achieved the desired effect, or the trouble she referred to resulted from the Voice, which she calls "the spent." Mary's dialogue could also suggest that she believes the poltergeist and Voice are the same entity, similar to the Bell Witch, which we will examine further in a future chapter. Mary's seeming contempt for the "priestly art" corroborates Catholic narratives that she never sincerely converted and that the supernatural problems and the Catholic Church's involvement were causing her marital issues. Finally, her opposition to the donation of family land provides a motive for the somewhat denigrating descriptions of her offered by some Catholic accounts. Dower rights would have entitled Mary to one-third of the estate, mentioned by Mary as "my lawful thirds." The letter indicates that she was suspicious of a Catholic-based confidence scheme threatening her inheritance.

Curiously, Anna Marshall's account, *Adam Livingston, the Wizard Clip, the Voice*, highlights Mary Livingston's letter but excludes its impetus. Mary's letter is in response to one published about a week earlier in the same newspaper by another priest. Intriguingly, this clergyman believed that the Wizard Clip affair was a hoax played on Adam by Mary for some unknown sinister reason and that "Gorman" and his unnamed mistress may be involved:[120]

> *Few there are in Martinsburg or Winchester but have heard of Livingston's ghosts and revelations. These seven or eight years past, this unaccountable imposture has been carried on by a man simple in appearance and his wife, who in my opinion is the ghost herself, and with the assistance of some other knavish hussies of the village, has played on the old man her husband. That the whole is imposture, whatever may be the motive of the actors, was thus discovered and is now made public as an homage due to truth.*
>
> *Went to see L. at W.C. Wonderful stories were told by this old man and wife, but unluckily for the reveling spirit, the wife of Gorman—the adulterer—is still alive. P. wrote to Dublin and found the woman alive, living with friends in the Parish of Caragh, near Naas. He has her letter where she claims G. as her husband.*
>
> *Let the public now judge who was the devil the burnt L.'s barn and played so many wicked pranks on his family. For my part, I am now satisfied that L's wife and G. and the hussy he keeps are and have been the chief actors in this unfavorable plot.*
>
> *L. Silo Phelan, Catholic Priest of Hagerstown*

A few other sources from the period mention Reverend Phelan. Sarah Brownstone revealed that Reverend Gallitzin had apparent difficulties with the Irish priest in her book *The Life of Demetrius Augustine Gallitzin: Prince and Priest*. He's also briefly noted in Shea's *History of the Catholic Church in the United States* for being arrested for conspiring to murder another priest named Fromm. Finally, Father Finotti's *The Mystery of the Wizard Clip* disregards part of Reverend Phelan's accusing letter:

> *Everything that the Voice predicted happened accordingly. It foretold that the wife of Gorman died in Ireland but, on account of the troubles she*

suffered in this world, went directly to Heaven. A Mr. Failin, a priest, said he wrote to Ireland concerning this fact and said she was not dead, but the Voice before he received his letter, admonished Livingston not to stagger in his faith that the letter was forged.

I can find no additional information about Mr. Gorman, why he might be considered a suspect in a hoax, or who his mistress was. Reverend Finotti's book mentions that "Mr. Goreman"[121] heard from the Voice three times in one week but nothing about what the Voice said. Based on the letters published in the *Potomak Guardian*, Mr. Gorman's involvement in the Wizard Clip legend was likely significant, but the available Catholic histories largely ignore it.

Reverend Phelan signed his letter as a Catholic priest from Hagerstown in 1798. Father Cahill, also of Hagerstown, was ministering to the Livingston family then. Reverend Cahill likely performed the exorcism, possibly with the help of Reverend Gallitzin, sometime after the autumn of 1797. He would be left thirty-four acres of Livingston's property ostensibly for this service five years later. Reverend Cahill built the log chapel at Hagerstown, the closest Catholic Church to Smithfield (Middleway) at the time. It was the only of its kind in Hagerstown, meaning that Phelan and Cahill both labored from this facility. Mr. Cahill returned to Ireland in 1806 and remained there until his death ten years later. That same year, Reverend Phelan offered to assist Reverend Gallitzin in Pennsylvania, which Dimitri abruptly declined. According to *The Life of Demetrius Augustine Gallitzin: Prince and Priest*, "The reverend gentleman who had already caused so much mischief, far more, it is to be hoped, that he knew or intended, continued to press his services, causing great annoyance to Dr. Gallitzin, and serving to keep alive the hostile feeling now nearly extinct." It is unclear if Reverend Phelan's accusations about the Wizard Clip being a hoax had caused ill will between these two clergymen. Nevertheless, their relationship ended entirely in 1806, according to Brownstone.

Regardless of Mary's protests, in 1802, Adam Livingston sold thirty-four acres of his property to Dennis Cahill and trustees for one dollar, intending the land to support a Catholic church. The details of the deed are as follows. Note that it does not mention a haunting or exorcism:

This indenture made the twenty-first day of February in the year one thousand eight hundred and two between Adam Levingston and Mary, his wife of Jefferson County Virginia of the first part, and the reverend Dennis

Adam Livingston plaque, Priest Field Pastoral Center. *Author's collection.*

Cahill of the same county of the second part and Richard McSherry, Joseph Minghini and Clement Pierce also of the same county of the third part. WHEREAS the said Denis Cahill is a regular clergyman of the Church of Rome and, by his exemplary conduct and punctual discharge of his duties belonging to the office, hath given particular pleasure to the said Adam Levingston, who is also of the same persuasion and is conscious on the said Reverend Dennis Cahill some lasting proof of his lasting esteem for him and the religion the principles of which he inculcates and enforces by his example. Now this Indenture witnesses that the said Adam Levingston and Mary his wife in consideration of the premises and of one-dollar current money of the United States of America and to him the said Adam in hand paid by the said Reverend Dennis Cahill at or before the sealing and delivery hereof the receipt whereof is hereby acknowledged and also in consideration of the sum of one-dollar like currently money to him and the said Adam Levingston in hand paid by the said Richard McSherry, Joseph Minghini and Clement Pierce at or before the sealing and delivery hereof the receipt whereof is hereby acknowledged have and each of them hath grated, bargained, sold, alienated, released and confirmed and by these presents the said Adam Levingston and Mary his wife to each of them doth grant, bargain, alien, release and confirm unto the said Richard McSherry, Joseph Minghini, and Clement Pierce and their heirs a certain tract or parcel of land...and all the houses, ways, buildings, improvements hereby conveyed belonging in anyway appertaining and the reversion and reversions remainder and remainders rents its use and profits thereof and also all the estate right interest claims and demand of the said Adam Levingston and

Mary his wife in and to the same to have and to hold the same land conveyed with the appurtenances unto the said Richard McSherry, Joseph Minghini, and Clement Pierce and their heirs to the only proper use and behoof of the said Richard McSherry, Joseph Minghini, and Clement Pierce and their heirs forever on upon this special trust and confidence that they said Richard McSherry, Joseph Minghini, and Clement Pierce do permit the said Reverend Dennis Cahill to reside upon the said tract of land and receive the whole emoluments arising there from without any account by him to be rendered and for his own use during the period of his natural life of the said Dennis Cahill without impeachment for waste and after the decease of the said reverend Dennis Cahill then to permit and suffer each clergyman of the same opinion in religion as shall meet with their approbation to hold and enjoy the same land and receive the emoluments arising there from during his natural life without any account to be rendered by him but calling thereupon and in the neighborhood thereof, and in case a Clergyman qualified as above and one will comply with the above conditions cannot be procured during every such interval said land is to be rented and the profits thereof are to be applied towards building and repatriating a church or chapel thereupon.

It is the design of the parties to these present that the trust hereby created shall extend to the survivor or the survivors of the said trustees and that

St. Michael's Basilica, Loretto, Pennsylvania. *Author's collection.*

Reverend Gallitzin founded St. Michael's Basilica. *Author's collection.*

the heirs of the last surviving trustee, that is, the trustee who lived longest, shall after his decease execute this trust and then the trust shall descend to their heirs and so on so there shall still be a trustee or trustees, but if by the changes in life, it shall turn out that all the inheritable blood which by this deed are made trustees fail then the court of the said county of Berkely are authorized to appoint three trustees so that they be members of the Church of Rome who when appointed shall have the same powers as the trustees first mentioned.[122]

Although he transferred thirty-four acres of his property to the Catholic Church in early 1802, Adam Livingston remained on his farm until March 1809, when he sold the rest of his Middleway property to brothers Joseph Bell Jr. and Benjamin Bell. At age seventy, Adam moved closer to some of his children and their families in Bedford County, Pennsylvania, where he stayed until his death in 1820. Father Gallitzin claimed to have kept in close touch with Adam, holding Mass at his home in Bedford "repeatedly." Adam's daughter, Mary, and her family became Reverend Gallitzin's church parishioners in Loretto, Pennsylvania, about twenty miles from Bedford.[123]

Chapter 4

THE VOICE AND THE ANGEL

Beloved, believe not every spirit, but try the spirits whether they are of God:
because many false prophets are gone out into the world.
—1 John 4:1

Unlike the secular versions, the unworldly events did not end with the exorcism in the Catholic Wizard Clip narratives; however, they are challenging to place in timeline order. It is also essential to preface this section by noting that nearly all of these post-exorcism details derive from members of the McSherry family. Father Gallitzin made a passing reference to the Voice in a letter to Anastasia's daughter, Catherine, claiming that it called her mother a "dear helpmate."[124] It is unclear if he heard this directly from the source or one of the witnesses. He admits to being "in possession of two letters which your pious mother wrote to one of her brothers, I think to Samuel Lilly, which contain some interesting facts and advice, communicated by Livingston to your mother by the Voice." Mary Livingston possibly referenced the Voice in her letter published in the *Potomak Guardian*. Almost all other accounts of the post-exorcism events originate from Anastasia McSherry, her daughter Ann and her granddaughter Helen Nicholson.

Shortly after the exorcism, a barefooted, poorly dressed man visited the family and instructed them in Catholicism. The man said, "I come to teach you the way to my father," and spent three days converting the family, after which he disappeared as he crossed a field in front of the house in full view of Adam Livingston, his daughters, and Rosa McSherry. From then on, Adam referred to this incident as a visit from an angel. The McSherry family–derived sources provide very little about this affair other than that the Livingstons provided him with shoes and the opportunity to shave. The visitor accepted the shoes but noted they were not needed where he is from, as it is neither hot nor cold there.[125]

Then one evening, after being a Catholic for several weeks, Mr. Livingston was startled by a shimmering light in the corner of his room. As the light grew in intensity, he began to hear a voice that explained that it came to instruct him in the sacraments of penance and Holy Eucharist. From then on, the Voice frequently manifested from a "brilliant light," according to accounts by Father Mulledy and the McSherry family. According to an 1872 letter from James Healy, bishop of Maine and New Hampshire, to Reverend Finotti, "Young people could see the author of the voice; older people could not." Additionally, it told Adam that it was once flesh and blood like him, and if he persevered, the spirit would reveal itself to him before Adam died. If it did, there is no record that I can find. Nor can I find a name or gender associated with the Voice other than speculation that it could be the dead Stranger or a priest because of its knowledge of the Catholic faith.[126]

Referring to the miraculous conversion of the Livingston family by the Angel and Voice, Reverend Mulledy noted that "it is…certain that no human person instructed them…they had no books in the house and had besides very little education in the English tongue."[127] Mulledy isn't the only researcher to suggest that the Livingstons were simple and spoke little English. Anna Marshall claimed that someone must have written Mary Livingston's letter to the *Potomak Guardian* for her because "they were not at home in the English language." Reverend Finotti stated that Prince Gallitzin was better suited to investigate the Livingston claims, as he spoke fluent German. However, I am skeptical that there was a problematic language barrier. While it is true that the family lived in a predominantly German-speaking community in Pennsylvania, Adam Livingston was born and raised in the British American colonies. He frequently visited his Virginian neighbors, the McSherrys and Minghinis, who presumably did not speak German. According to the Finotti and Marshall accounts, Mary Livingston's closest friends were likely of English descent, as they were Quakers. None of the sources mentions what language the Voice spoke when instructing the family, but a few state that it would sing hymns in Latin and English. Most curiously, these accounts overlook Dennis Cahill, an Irishman who, according to the eyewitness Dimitri Gallitzin, cleansed the house of evil spirits and "took them into the church."

Almost all Catholic Wizard Clip histories and allegories depict the disembodied Voice as sweet and supportive, but I would argue the opposite. While fully acknowledging the temporal and cultural differences that may influence my interpretation of the alleged events versus that of the authors, I feel justified in stating that the Voice as a story character is just as terrifying as the poltergeist, if they are separate entities at all. Later, I will compare the Wizard Clip story to similar folktales that include a disembodied voice and poltergeist-like activities but are not different characters.

These Catholic histories and fables claim that the Voice was "always helpful" and credit it and the Angel with instructing and converting the Livingston family to Catholicism rather than Father Cahill, whom Adam admired so much that he donated property. In my opinion, the stories paint the Voice as demanding, condescending, spiteful, and frightening. It also had extraordinary powers, such as reading minds, the ability to bilocate, predicting the future, and making things invisible. Finally, despite Catholic depictions of this spirit being helpful, the poltergeist activity did not end with its manifestation.

CONTINUING PHYSICAL DISTURBANCES

Early in the Voice's tenure, probably in the fall of 1797 or 1798, it ordered the family to fast for forty days, with at least three hours of prayer each day, primarily for souls in Purgatory. It repeated this in the winter during Lent, ordering the family to pray every night until it said amen.[128] Like earlier, when the poltergeist kept the family sleep-deprived, the Voice would regularly wake them up at night, demanding, "I want prayers!"[129] According to Mrs. McSherry's granddaughter:

The voice would often wake everyone in the house three times a night for prayers. Just as one of the daughters, irritated by the nightly harassment, began to think that the tormented souls in Purgatory probably deserved their torment, as they could have saved themselves, the disembodied spirit began to scream for help. The girls asked how they could assist, to which the spirit replied, "Prayers, for we are in excruciating torment. Hand me something, and you will be convinced." The terrified girl held up a freshly laundered shirt, to which a flaming hand immediately burned a distinct handprint.[130]

"The Flaming Hand." *Lucy Elliot.*

Although less menacing than decapitating livestock and burning beds and barns, the Voice continued to harass the family in ways reminiscent of the poltergeist events before the exorcism. On another dark evening, a different voice shrieked for help, burning the letters "I.H.S." and a cross shape into a goatskin vest. This time the Voice said it was a dead relative of Adam named Catherine Gookman and that she was suffering in the flames of Purgatory. It is unclear if this was a different spirit or if the Voice mimicked Adam's relative.[131]

In addition to the weird happenings at the Livingstons, poltergeist activity began to affect the McSherry residence after the exorcism. One afternoon, shortly after placing her slumbering infant son in his cradle, Mrs. McSherry terrifyingly watched as it began to rock violently. The Voice later told Mr. Livingston that the devil was trying to destroy the child, as he knew the boy would become his enemy one day. That boy eventually grew to become Reverend William McSherry, provincial superior of the Society of Jesus (Jesuits) in the United States and the eighteenth president of Georgetown College, mentioned earlier.[132] Another event occurred at the Livingston residence involving possibly the same infant:

> One night while Adam and his daughter Charlotte were relaxing, the voice manifested once again as a bright light in the corner of the room. It came to tell Charlotte that the devil had been trying to tempt her all day, but the innocence of a neighbor's baby [whom she had looked after that day] had protected her.[133]

The poltergeist activity returned on another evening when a Methodist preacher asked for lodging at the McSherry residence during a thunderstorm. Mrs. McSherry hospitably arranged for the man to stay in the bedroom often used by visiting priests and where church vestments were stored. Later, the McSherrys were kept awake all night by loud unattributable footsteps in the house, including their bedroom. Concerned that their guest was also disturbed by the strange sounds, they inquired the following day, but the Protestant minister said he slept very well. Adam Livingston arrived soon after the preacher left with news from the Voice. It said that God had permitted the disturbance to punish them for harboring a minister of the devil in a place where they keep sacred things.[134]

On a Thursday back at the Livingstons, Mary Livingston prepared "an abundant amount of meat soup from which there was plenty left over" after dinner. She hid it in the cellar to serve it to her family the next day. However,

Methodist church, Middleway, West Virginia. *Author's collection.*

the next morning, the pot's contents were plain water. The Voice suddenly and piercingly chastised Mary, claiming responsibility for the missing soup and demanding that if she did not submit to the Catholic Church's rules, she would one day open her eyes to the flames of Hell.[135]

The Voice constantly warned the Livingstons and wealthy McSherrys against vanity. According to Anastasia McSherry, the Voice scorned "sinful worms of the earth" that bedecked and adorned their wicked bodies. She also noted that it preached that Satan invented ruffles, fringes, flounces, tuckers, and modesty pieces and forbade cutting or curling of hair.[136] This anecdote is intriguing, as Richard McSherry was known to dress carefully in the fashion of his day "with lace ruffles, powdered hair, and silver knee

"Shattered Mirror." *Lucy Elliot.*

buckles."[137] The Voice declared that "thousands of people were burning in hell forever because of grievous sins resulting from their wishing to follow the fashions of the world." The spirit became incensed one evening as three McSherry girls tried on dresses. It violently shattered their floor-length mirror and loudly rebuked the terrified youths about their lack of modesty.[138]

From here, the haunting seems to progress beyond an infestation, even though an exorcism had allegedly occurred. I am not qualified to make this claim with any authority. I am merely commenting on the similarity of some post-exorcism events to the signs and factors of obsession and possession according to the Catholic classification system for demonic physical attacks provided by Raphael Brown's 1949 pamphlet on the Wizard Clip. None of the Catholic sources claims that the Wizard Clip haunting progressed beyond infestation. Still, Mary Livingston maintained that "the trouble still remains in Livingston's family, at times to a greater or less degree, despite Priestly art" at least a year after the exorcism allegedly took place.

The Voice began to cause physical pain. Mr. Livingston's son refused to perform his reaping chores one harvest season unless his father paid him regular harvest wages. Soon afterward, he became afflicted by a painfully swollen and infected knee that kept him bedridden for a year and a half. The Voice finally announced, "He has satisfied the Justice of God for his disobedience and disrespect to his father," and the young man became miraculously well again.[139]

Adam suddenly doubled over in pain while working in the crop fields on another afternoon. When his sons rolled him over, they were taken aback by how pale Mr. Livingston had become. As they helped the sobbing man to his feet, he revealed how he was overcome by another dreadful shriek from a lost soul in Purgatory, crying out for help.[140] Another time, an entire arm manifested and forcefully struck Adam. The source of this detail, Anastasia McSherry, provides no reason for the attack; however, this abuse falls within the obsession category definition.[141]

Making Known Distant and Hidden Things

After the fiery hand incident, the Voice read people's thoughts more frequently, discussed simultaneous events occurring in other locations, and began predicting the future. Many similar historical and folkloric examples of prophecy and bilocation claims exist that are almost always associated with witchcraft or divine miracles. At Salem in 1692, Reverend George

Burrows stood trial for killing several soldiers "by the agency of his shape."[142] These men were away fighting natives and almost certainly died in battle. Likewise, bilocation is a miracle associated with many Catholic saints, such as Drogo and Martin de Porres. I raise this point to show that although the Voice's ability to make known distant and hidden things could indicate that the haunting was progressing toward possession, the Catholic authors of this portion of the legend believed that the Voice's abilities were a miracle.

The Voice reprimanded Eve Livingston for committing the "great sin" of weeping at a Protestant meeting. Eve went to an unnamed Protestant church shortly after converting to Catholicism and became overwhelmed with emotion while thinking that its members were "astray, not knowing anything of the Catholic Church." The Voice said that the Protestants thought Eve was affected by what she heard, as they did not know her thoughts and forbade her from going again. During another late-night prayer session commanded by the Voice, one of Livingston's girls failed to mention a specific sin out of shame; the Voice told the entire family and ordered her to confess as soon as possible.[143]

Mr. Livingston visited the McSherrys one morning to inform them that the Voice claimed that Mrs. McSherry's sister, Mrs. Spaulding, who lived in Baltimore, had passed away the previous night (December 15, 1801). The Voice said that she needed Masses, as she was in Purgatory for overindulgence with her children. A letter confirming the death came several days later. Mrs. McSherry followed the voice's instruction, having eighty Masses said for her sister. One afternoon shortly after this, Mr. and Mrs. McSherry visited the Livingstons, and as they walked onto the property, the gate and door to the home opened without anyone touching them. The Voice explained (through Adam Livingston) that Mrs. Spaulding opened them in gratitude for their help.[144] The Voice also claimed to know about the death of Mrs. Goreman in Ireland, although Reverend Phelan seemingly debunked this claim.

The Voice became adept at predicting the future and often spoke of troubles yet to come. One day, it instructed Adam Livingston to inform Mrs. McSherry that although she would not live to see it, War, Pestilence, and Famine would visit her children. It added that these scourges would not touch those that remained faithful. According to Anastasia McSherry's granddaughter, this proved true, as none of the eight children suffered the slightest injury during the Civil War except for one son who died from overexertion while working in a military hospital.[145]

The Voice predicted that Mrs. Livingston would die in her home; therefore, whenever Mrs. Livingston became ill, she would stay with her friends, a neighboring Quaker family. On one of these occasions, a daughter of this family also became deathly sick and, knowing about the supernatural happenings, asked Mrs. Livingston for spiritual guidance. The Voice told Mary that the child needed baptism, but Mary refused to become involved. After the girl died, the Voice derided Mrs. Livingston's cowardice and loudly proclaimed that this transgression would appear against her on Judgment Day. As predicted, Mrs. Livingston passed in her home a few years later.[146] The Voice also warned Mrs. McSherry that her brother, studying to be a priest at Georgetown, would die a blasphemer. Mrs. McSherry's granddaughter Helen later described how this prophecy materialized, as her relative lost faith and died in sin after falling from a horse.[147]

According to Joseph Mobberly's account, the voice prophesied that Mrs. Minghini would convert to Catholicism with the help of Mrs. McSherry.[148] Interestingly, this tale is similar to the story of the Stranger and may be its impetus. In this version, Mr. Minghini is a lapsed Catholic who refused to send for a priest for his dying Protestant wife even though she requested the last rites. Like Adam Livingston in the Stranger narrative, Mr. Minghini allegedly gave the excuse that there was no priest within forty miles, which was likely true, as Hagerstown is about thirty-six miles from Middleway. In this story, Mrs. McSherry went to Mrs. Minghini, prayed an act of contrition with her, and, with the help of one of the Livingston children, found a priest who arrived in time. The woman died but went to Purgatory instead of Hell, according to the Voice.

Referring to the property Adam Livingston donated, the Voice foretold, "Before the end of time, this will be a great place of prayer, fasting, and praise."[149] After over one hundred years of disuse, Bishop Denis O'Connell of Richmond obtained a court decision validating the church's claim to the property in 1922.[150] Another fifty-plus years passed before the Priest Field Pastoral Center finally opened, seemingly fulfilling the Voice's prophecy.[151]

CASTING JUDGMENT

The Voice could be vindictive at times. An unnamed Protestant wife of another Catholic man, this time in Winchester, also allegedly asked for a priest when she was near death. A messenger rode to the McSherry estate and found an unnamed priest. However, when the priest went to gather his horse, named Old Bull, from the McSherry farm's modest-sized "spring pasture," the steed was nowhere to be found. After everyone searched for the animal without success, Mr. McSherry had one of his horses readied for the priest, and he left after a considerable delay. Soon after, Old Bull began neighing and was found in the middle of the spring pasture, to the utter amazement of the thirty persons who had searched for him. The Voice then admitted to Mr. Livingston that the priest's mount was made invisible, hindering his ability to oversee the woman's deathbed conversion and provide last rites because she had put off her conversion until the last minute.[152]

Contrastingly, the Voice would help those it deemed worthy of redemption. Mr. McSherry nearly died of severe illness in 1804. He had avoided confession and communion for some time due to an undisclosed disagreement with Reverend Cahill. The Voice commanded Mr. Livingston to visit the dying man and deliver a message that he would be cured if he humbled himself to the church. Mr. McSherry immediately sent a messenger for his priest, even though his family felt it was too late. None expected Mr. McSherry to live through the night. Father Cahill sped back to the McSherry Farm and administered the last rites to the struggling gentleman, after which he drifted into a labored sleep. The following day, the entire house awoke suddenly to the scream of one of the daughters. When she saw Richard walking about the house in the predawn hours, she had mistaken his pale and emaciated form for a ghost. Mr. McSherry was cured and lived until September 7, 1822.[153]

From here, news of the Voice and its activities becomes sporadic. Mr. Livingston donated the property that would become Priest Field two years before Richard McSherry's miraculous healing. Five years later, Adam would leave Middleway altogether.[154] No further record of the events is available, but Catholic versions claim that the Voice remained with Adam for seventeen years, until about 1814–15.[155] There is no mention of why it left when it did. Adam died in Pennsylvania in 1820. Although there doesn't appear to be a record of the final ten years with the Voice, news continued to spread about the legend. An article in the *Richmond Enquirer* on January 11, 1831, detailed a spat in the House of Delegates when Representative John Gallaher of Jefferson County took offense when another Representative named Mr. Leigh asked if Smithfield was once called Wizard Clip.[156] Mr. Leigh assured the gentleman that he meant no insult and wished the name had stuck: "There was a Smithfield here and a Smithfield there—they were to be found everywhere—but there was not another Wizard's Clip in the whole country." Mr. Gallaher also claimed to have owned a pamphlet "about the subject of the clippings by Prince Gallitzin," corroborating the priest's claim that he wrote an account.

Chapter 5

RELIGIOUS-HISTORICAL CONTEXT

I watched with glee
While your kings and queens
Fought for ten decades
For the gods they made.
—"Sympathy for the Devil," the Rolling Stones

Having established that belief in witchcraft, necromancy, and poltergeists are part and parcel of the Wizard Clip legend, it would be helpful to briefly examine the religious and historical context from which that belief system formed. This chapter is by no means a comprehensive look at everything that may have influenced the formation of this folklore, but it will provide some background, starting with its root, sorcery. Folklorist Gerald Milnes described four forms of witchcraft in his book *Signs Cures & Witchery: German Appalachian Folklore*. The oldest formed from fertility cults that attempted to aid the fertilization of crops and the impregnation of livestock through occultic measures. This practice also gave rise to midwives and herbal healers. The second form materialized in the late Middle Ages from Western European Christian sects that began to accuse these same folks and others on the fringe of society as devil-worshiping heathens who could draw on the dark forces of Hell to attack others. By the early modern period, Protestants and Catholics had become engrossed with the witch hunt craze, especially in German-speaking lands. Many early eighteenth-century Appalachian German immigrants were direct descendants of the people affected by this era. The third form grew out of the first two and is still represented by folk magic practitioners in Appalachia today. The main difference in this form is that the witch can consciously choose to use good white magic or evil black magic. This form contrasts with the previous one, which assumes that a demon or the devil himself compelled the witch to perform crimes and acts of heresy. The final form, neopaganism, came from the new age movement and is only tangentially related to the others.[157]

In some Christian circles, anxiety about witchcraft remains deep-seated, but this seemingly irrational fear likely formed from preservation needs long forgotten. As with unprovoked stresses triggered by serpents or darkness, these fears safeguard cultures against something shocking but probably misremembered. On average, five people die annually from a venomous snake bite in the United States. Cows kill more than four times that number, but bovinophobia is not prevalent among Americans. Most Americans never suffer a snake bite, but a third of the adult population is ophidiophobic.[158] I assume the influence of Christianity may account for this disproportion, as Genesis tells us that a serpent tricked Adam and Eve, causing their banishment from Eden. Likewise, I assume that most people who genuinely fear sorcery have never encountered a witch, as described by the Old Testament. Nonetheless, the belief remains in pockets of Western Christian culture today.

For example, residents of Lowellville, Ohio, near the Appalachian foothills, have burned in effigy a feminine figure most years since 1895, deemed the "Baby Doll Dance." Lowellville's residents of Catholic Italian heritage began the tradition because they believed that burning her cleansed the town's sins.[159] This tradition is mainly nostalgic; however, in 2022, I fielded several complaints about the theme of the fall folklore festival I host annually in western Pennsylvania, about twenty miles from Lowellville. Our featured guest, Thomas White, agreed to emcee a discussion about his fascinating book, *The Witch of the Monongahela: Folk Magic in Early Western Pennsylvania*. Even after several social media posts and a radio interview explaining that the festival celebrates folklore and that we were not endorsing the dark arts, our musical guest declined our invite, citing concerns about the event's subject matter. Event attendance was the lowest on record. While some Appalachians almost certainly fear witchcraft because of their faith, history provides another reason for the subliminal wariness associated with sorcery: the early modern European witch craze.[160]

Witch prosecution in Europe did not gain momentum until Catholic inquisitors and Protestant reformers began using it as a weapon in the sixteenth century. Initially, the Inquisition was a method to purge heretics from the Catholic Church, but Pope John XXII broadened its mandate to include those who practiced black magic. In 1320, he granted the Dominicans the authority to hunt sorcerers. Inquisitors of varying groups used witchcraft accusations to silence religious dissenters such as the Waldensians,[161] rival orders within the church such as the Knights Templar, and even Catholic political opponents like Joan of Arc. However, witch trials were still rare across Europe before the Reformation began. German Catholic clergyman Heinrich Kramer published the most infamous anti-sorcery treatise in 1486, the *Malleus Maleficarum*, or *Hammer of Witches*, setting the conditions to ignite the witch-hunting powder keg.[162]

By this time, belief in witchcraft was widespread in Europe, but prosecutions rarely resulted in an execution. That would change in the mid-sixteenth century as Catholics and Protestants used the *Malleus Maleficarum* and other quasi-legal authorities to cleanse their populaces and purge their opponents. At the time, Protestants and Catholics rarely agreed on anything. However, the evils of witchcraft were not a point of contention. Martin Luther preached that the "devil's whores" could steal milk, raise storms, and torture babies. He approved the execution of accused witches, claiming, "I should have no compassion on these witches. I would burn them all." John Calvin, the preeminent leader of the Reformed Protestant movement, once preached, "Let us note that if we want to be taken for Christians, witchcrafts, enchantments, and such other similar things must be no more tolerated among us than robbers and murderers. In accordance with Exodus, a witch must be slain."[163]

Many Christian theologians contributed literature that fed the witchcraft hysteria. Jesuit Martin Del Rio's 1599 *Disquisitiones Magicae* (*Magical Investigations*) reinvigorated old ideas from the *Malleus Maleficarum*—historians credit Del Rio with bringing witch-burning to European Low Countries. Seven years before the book's publication, Del Rio persecuted Catholic priest and theologian Cornelius Loos, the first of the denomination to publish a book doubting the existence of witchcraft and the reliability of confessions made under torture. Loos was thrown in prison, likely tortured, and forced to recant.[164] Another witchcraft theoretician, Benedikt Carpzov—a Lutheran lawyer, judge, and law professor—published *Practica Rerum Criminalium* in 1635, promoting using torture during witch trials to solicit confessions. Carpzov is likely indirectly responsible for the deaths

Left: Portrait of young John Calvin. *Library of Geneva, Wikimedia Commons, PD-US.*

Below: King James Bible. *Author's collection.*

of more than twenty thousand people convicted of witchcraft.[165] A list of similar authors is too long to include in this brief synopsis, but one stands out above all the rest. King James I is most remembered for the English colonization of North America and for authorizing the most widely printed book in history, the King James Bible. Before this, as King James VI of Scotland, he established his demon-hunting credentials by writing *Daemonologie*, published in 1597, ten years before the settlement of the Virginia colony named for him.[166] He described his motivations for writing the book on its first page:

> *The fearful abounding at this time in this country of these detestable slaves of the Devil, the Witches or enchanters, has moved me (beloved reader) to dispatch in post, this following treatise of mine. It is written not in any way (as I protest) to serve for a show of my learning and intelligence, but only (moved of conscience) by this means, so far as I can, to resolve the doubting hearts of many; both that such assaults of Satan are most certainly practiced, and that the instruments thereof, merit most severely to be punished.*
>
> *I am against the damnable opinions of two principally in our age, whereof the one called Scot an Englishman is not ashamed in public print to deny that there can be such a thing as witchcraft and so maintains the old error of the Sadducees, the denial of spirits. The other, called Weyer, a German Physician, sets out a public apology for all the people of such craft, whereby, procuring for their impunity, he plainly betrays himself to have been one of that profession.*
>
> *And to make this treatise more pleasant and simple to read, I have put it in the form of a dialogue, which I have divided into three books: The first speaks of magic in general, and especially necromancy. The second of sorcery and witchcraft: the third contains a discourse of all these kinds of spirits and specters that appear and trouble people.*
>
> *My intention in this labor is to prove two things, as I have already said: First, such devilish arts have been and continue to exist, and second, what exact trial and punishment they deserve.[167]*

King James ruled during a tumultuous era of the Reformation. At thirteen months old, he became king of Scotland when his Catholic mother, Mary Queen of Scots, was forced by Protestant lords to abdicate. Her cousin Queen of England Elizabeth I eventually ordered her beheading for treason. Elizabeth's father, Henry VIII, initiated the

English Reformation when the pope refused to annul his marriage to his first wife, Catherine of Aragon. Elizabeth's Catholic half-sister preceded her reign and became known as Bloody Mary for her attempts to restore Catholic rule in England, during which she burned almost three hundred Protestants at the stake.

James succeeded his cousin Elizabeth, becoming ruler of Scotland, England, and Ireland in 1603. The following year, Parliament enacted his Witchcraft Act of 1604, also known by its full title, *An Act Against Conjuration, Witchcraft and Dealing with Evil and Wicked Spirits*.[168] This law codified two degrees of criminal witchcraft. Those accused of first-degree witchcraft faced the death penalty for many reasons, including causing death or destruction through the conjuration of an evil spirit. Second-degree witchcraft activities included mystic services such as brewing love potions or divining the location of lost or buried treasure, and those accused faced a year in prison.

In 1605, King James survived a Catholic assassination attempt called the Gunpowder Plot, or the Jesuit Treason. This event spurred anti-Catholic sentiment in the realm for hundreds of years. The English still celebrate Guy Fawkes Night on the fifth of November, commemorating the failed plot with bonfires and fireworks, although anti-Catholic sentiments are no longer the focus. The American colonies observed November 5 as an anti-Catholic holiday called Pope's Night, but most abandoned the custom during the American Revolution.

As he documented in the preface of *Daemonologie*, King James wrote the book in response to publications skeptical of supernatural happenings. According to tradition, James even ordered his subjects to burn all copies of Reginald Scot's 1584 book, *The Discoverie of Witchcraft*. However, several historians doubt the veracity of this claim. An English member of Parliament, Scot believed that the prosecution of witches was irrational and, in the book, blamed the Catholic Church for the witch trial hysteria. The other author specifically mentioned by King James, Johann Weyer, published in 1563 *On the Illusions of the Demons and on Spells and Poisons*, in which he is the first to suggest that those confessing to sorcery may be mentally ill.

Like Cotton Mather and his work *Wonders of the Invisible World*, King James may have written *Daemonologie* to justify his role in presiding over witch trials, specifically the North Berwick Trials that occurred in Scotland from 1590 to 1591. The king interrogated several of the more than one hundred suspected witches during these proceedings. James became motivated by a terrible storm he experienced in 1590 on the way back to

Portrait of King
James I of England
and Scotland. *Daniel
Mytens, National
Portrait Gallery
(London), Wikimedia
Commons, PD-US.*

Scotland after marrying his wife, Anne, in Denmark. Although the king
and queen survived, six women from Copenhagen confessed under torture
to raising the storm to kill the queen and her new husband. When the king
learned of this, he launched the North Berwick tribunal. Those executed
had confessed under torture to attempting to harm the king through pacts
with the devil.[169]

In *Daemonologie*, King James described how witches had the power to
cause sickness and death, drive people mad, raise storms, and direct spirits
to haunt individuals or places. He believed that the only remedy for the evil
doings of witches was their apprehension, conviction, and swift execution.
He endorsed water tests, or ducking, as a means of discovering witches and
wrote that river waters would refuse to receive to their bosom the bodies of

"Ducking a Witch." *Lucy Elliot.*

people who had shaken off the sacred water of the baptism, meaning that if they floated, they were a witch. James advocated using torture to acquire confessions and deemed it legitimate to accept the testimony of children to convict a witch because God would not allow the slandering of innocent by witchcraft allegations.[170] This specific belief would heavily influence the Puritan prosecutors in Salem in 1692. Later, James would become more skeptical, but his work inspired clerics and theologians such as Joseph Glanville, Cotton Mather, and William Perkins to continue anti-witchcraft crusades for decades.

Europe's Wars of Religion began in 1522, shortly after the issuance of the Edict of Worms,[171] and lasted until the end of the Thirty Years' War in 1648. The Thirty Years' War was one of Europe's longest and most destructive. It began when Lutherans threw two Catholic governors out of a castle window in Prague during the Counterreformation. The war started as a civil conflict within the Holy Roman Empire but grew to include most of Europe. The lands that would become Germany suffered the most during the conflict. Battles and sieges reduced entire city-states to almost nothing. For example, in 1631, forces from the Holy Roman Empire and Catholic League laid siege to the Protestant town of Magdeburg. The city had a prewar population of 30,000, but a census recorded 449 residents one year later. The final assault on the city breached its defenses, burning 1,700 of Magdeburg's 1,900 buildings. More than 20,000 of its residents died. Likewise, witch trials continued to be a useful political tool for rulers during the conflict. About 900 people were burned at the stake as part of the Counterreformation by Prince-Bishop Adolf von Ehrenberg of Wurzburg from 1626 to 1631. Another 900 burned in Bamberg at roughly the same time.[172]

Most witch hunt executions in central Europe occurred between the onset of the Counterreformation and the end of the Thirty Years' War. During this time, cities, principalities, and kingdoms could change from Catholic to Protestant or vice versa virtually overnight due to political instability and the lack of separation of church and state. Witch trials became a valuable tool to silence partisans. Over the course of events, authorities executed at least 100,000 people in the land that would eventually become Germany, with the last occurring in 1775. The specific area of Germany from which the Livingston family emigrated was, in many ways, the epicenter of witch hysteria and persecution in Europe. In their book *Witchcraft and Magic in Europe: The Period of the Witch Trials*, Bengt Ankarloo and Stuart Clark identify the area of southwestern Germany as the "most severe" regarding witch hunts during that time. Germany had what Ankarloo and Clark coined as "super hunts" due to the unprecedented number of accused and executed. The severity of hunts in this area eventually garnered official condemnations from other religious leaders and influenced future laws regarding witch trials.[173]

Philosophical trends began to reject religion's role in secular affairs in the decades following the Thirty Years' War, giving rise to the Enlightenment. Many Enlightenment philosophers blamed superstitious belief as being the cause of so much suffering during Europe's Wars of Religion. Voltaire, French Enlightenment philosopher and friend of Reverend Gallitzin's parents, once claimed, "Never has there been a more universal empire than that of the Devil. What can dethrone him? Reason." France repealed its witchcraft laws in 1682, followed by Prussia in 1714 and Britain in 1736.[174] English Enlightenment-era philosopher John Locke's argument for the separation of church and state would later influence Thomas Jefferson, author of the Virginia Statute for Religious Freedom:

> *Once you allow that civil governments can enforce religious uniformity among their citizens, you have conceded the same right to London, Geneva, and Rome. But it is clear that these places hold different religions to be the true one, in which case it follows that you have conceded the right of forced uniformity to false religions as well as the true one. What makes such a position doubly ridiculous is that people's eternal fate is solely dependent on the place of their birth or residence rather than on the intrinsic or proven truth of their religious allegiance.*[175]

Outside of Salem, witch-hunting hysteria didn't take hold in the American colonies. Still, there were a few notable cases. In 1684, William Penn presided over a trial in which neighbors accused a Finnish woman named Margaret Mattson from Pennsylvania's New Sweden settlement of violating King James's 1604 Witchcraft Act by bewitching cattle and other similar charges. Penn dismissed the case, allegedly coyly stating that Pennsylvania has no law against riding a broom. He found her guilty of having a witch's reputation and ordered her to practice good behavior.[176]

In the Virginia colony, the people of Pungo accused Grace Sherwood of witchcraft multiple times.[177] Grace was a folk healer and midwife, but more importantly, she was a widow who inherited her late husband's farm and did not get along with neighbors who likely had an interest in her property. After several accusations—including killing livestock and crops

by incantation, transforming into a black cat, and causing a miscarriage—Grace underwent a trial by ducking in 1706. The magistrates followed King James's instructions for water testing a witch. They declared that if Sherwood floated, she would be deemed guilty; if she did not, she would be innocent. Six men bound her with rope and tied her right thumb to her left big toe and her left thumb to her right big toe; then she was rowed out and cast into a river, where she quickly floated to the surface. The sheriff then tied

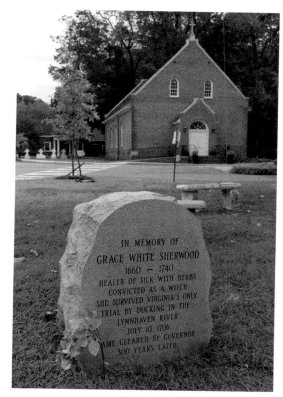

IN MEMORY OF
GRACE WHITE SHERWOOD
1660 – 1740
HEALER OF SICK WITH HERBS
CONVICTED AS A WITCH
SHE SURVIVED VIRGINIA'S ONLY
TRIAL BY DUCKING IN THE
LYNNHAVEN RIVER
JULY 10, 1706
AME CLEARED BY GOVERNOR
300 YEARS LATER

Opposite: Grace Sherwood's statue. *Author's collection.*

Left: Old Donation Episcopal Church. *Author's collection.*

Below: Witch Duck Point neighborhood. *Author's collection.*

Witch Duck Bay. *Author's collection.*

Witchduck Road, Virginia Beach. *Author's collection.*

a thirteen-pound Bible around her neck, causing her to sink, but she untied herself and returned to the surface, convincing many spectators that she was a witch. She was convicted, sentenced to jail, and forfeited her property. Grace would eventually be set free after almost eight years of incarceration. Three hundred years later, in July 2006, Virginia's Governor Kaine granted a pardon to "officially restore the good name of Grace Sherwood." The town erected a statue in her honor.

In Philadelphia, a mob lynched an elderly German woman nicknamed "Korbmacher" (basket weaver) in 1787 for witchcraft a few blocks from the Constitutional Convention, and she later died from her injuries. The mob believed she caused a child to become sick and die "under the malignant influence of a charm."[178] During the Wizard Clip haunting, a Charleston, South Carolina newspaper reported in 1793 that an enslaved person was tried for witchcraft, condemned, and hanged.[179] Still, American Enlightenment ideals were taking hold in society by this time. Adam Jortner, author of *Blood from the Sky: Miracles and Politics in the Early American Republic*, noted, "Modern evangelicalism is much more attuned to the presence of miracles and the supernatural in modern life than were most Protestant varietals of the early republic." For example, when discussions about the New Madrid Earthquakes in the House of Representatives trended toward supernatural causation in 1812, John C. Calhoun decried:

> *I did hope that the age of superstition was passed and that no attempt would be made to influence the measures of government, which ought to be founded in wisdom and policy, by the vague, I may say superstitious, feelings of any man, whatever may be the physical appearances which give rise to them….It would mark a fearful retrograde in civilization; it would prove a dreadful declination toward barbarism.*[180]

Supreme Court justice Joseph Story wrote that the Salem Witch Trials derived "partly from credulity, and partly from overwhelming fraud, in 1828. The whole of these proceedings exhibits melancholy proofs of the effect of superstition in darkening the mind." In his 1829 *Lecture on Popular Superstition*, Unitarian minister Bernard Whitman noted, "If people believe the devil works miracles, that witches exist," or that "religious excitements and commotions of the present day are occasioned by the miraculous effusions of the holy spirit," then "trials for heresy blasphemy and witchcraft would once more disgrace the annals of our nation."[181]

During this brief juncture in American history, belief in witchcraft waned as a Protestant spiritual revival began. Tolerance for non-Protestant ideas like a Purgatorial spirit's ability to influence the living helped to popularize poltergeist stories. These elements combined to conceive two unique American legends: the Wizard Clip and the Bell Witch. In both cases, the people affected likely believed that a witch was tormenting them. However, because these stories did not achieve widespread popularity until the Spiritualism movement was at its peak, we now interpret them as ghost stories. In the next chapter, we will explore other influences on the formation of these uncommon legends.

Chapter 6

A LEGEND FORMS

Priests and conjurors are of the same trade.
—*Thomas Paine*, The Age of Reason

The religious-historical context reveals what European immigrants in Appalachia likely thought about government, religion, and the occult at the onset of the newly forming nation. This chapter will discuss how an older legend, the Devil of Glenluce, probably influenced Wizard Clip storytellers. It will further discuss how belief in witchcraft and poltergeist phenomena traveled with immigrants and their offspring as they migrated west, helping shape America's unique hybrid witch-ghost story, the Bell Witch. Then, after a period of obscurity, a filmmaker from Maryland would revive the genre with massive success at the end of the twentieth century by creating *The Blair Witch Project*. First, a look at the primary authors and the timeframe in which they penned their accounts reveals the possible motivations behind some of the Wizard Clip legend's underlying themes. The chief cause appears to be competition. Competition with popular Protestant developments, Enlightenment-era governance, and the rise of Spiritualism inspired Catholic writers responsible for the legend's formation.

COMPETITION WITH PROTESTANTS AND GOVERNANCE

Some Catholics likely found utility in using the Wizard Clip story for its propaganda value during the church's early history in the United States. The prominent underlying themes of the early Catholic Wizard Clip narratives are anti-Protestant and counter-Enlightenment. The Enlightenment movement undermined religion's political and social control influence in the governance of nations, and it was especially critical of Catholicism. Reverend Gallitzin's departure from Europe at the onset of the Reign of Terror almost certainly prejudiced him against Enlightenment thinking, which becomes evident in his later writings.[182] An excellent example is Reverend Gallitzin's *Letter to a Protestant Clergyman*, a 178-page text he wrote in 1820 defending Catholic principles. In it, Dimitri uses the Wizard Clip story to criticize the Reformation, the Enlightenment, the doctrine for the cessation of miracles, and Adam Livingston's former Protestant clergy:

> *I am acquainted with a very respectable man, formerly a Protestant, whom this acknowledged want of power in his minister caused to forsake the pretended Reformation and, with his whole family, to embrace the Catholic faith. For a considerable length of time, he was persecuted and his property destroyed by the agency of evil spirits. The clothes belonging to him and his family were seen (by invisible hands) cutting to pieces, stones were seen moving across the room (held by invisible hands), fire burst repeatedly from out of their beds in broad daylight, strange and frightful apparitions, and strange noises terrified them very often at night.*
>
> *The good man reading in his bible that Christ had given his ministers power over evil spirits started from home to Winchester in Virginia, and having, with tears in his eyes, related to his minister (parson S____t) the history of his distress, losses, and sufferings begged of him to come to his house and exercise in his favor the power he had received from Jesus Christ. The parson candidly confessed that he had no such power. The good old man insisted that he must have that power, for he found it in the bible. The parson replied that that power existed only in old times but was done away with now. The old man, although living in this Enlightened age, had not sagacity enough to understand the distinction between old times and new times, but according to your minister's rule, he believed nothing but what he found contained in his Bible. He, therefore, concluded that parson S____t could not be a minister of Christ, and having left him, he applied to other persons calling themselves ministers of Christ, some of whom promised relief. They came, prayed, and read, but they prayed and read in vain. Finally, the old man having (through the means of a respectable Catholic neighbor) obtained the assistance of a real minister of Christ, found the relief for which he prayed so fervently and soon after became a most edifying member of the Catholic Church.*

Your minister would laugh heartily if you should relate to him the above facts; for with the wise men of this Enlightened age, he has peremptorily decided that miracles, etc., etc., are no longer necessary and, of course, have ceased—since when I did not learn, nor did I ever find any passage in Scripture which authorizes the belief that miracles should ever cease altogether, or that Evil Spirits should never more have it in their power to molest the bodies, and the property of men, as they used to during the lifetime of our Savior, and after His Resurrection.

Thousands of the most respectable, the most learned, the most holy of our Missionaries, in all the different parts of the globe, met with numberless instances of this kind, especially among infidels, and had as many opportunities of exercising in their favor the power which Jesus Christ granted his apostles over Evil Spirits, which power had descended to their successors. [183]

The young former aristocrat, whose parents' close acquaintances included Enlightenment elites like Voltaire and Diderot, evidently found validation for his youthful rebellious conversion to Roman Catholicism by investigating the miraculous aspects of the Wizard Clip mystery. Although religious tolerance was the groundwork of the new nation, other early Catholic Church leaders also likely cautiously watched America's enlightened founders and philosophers. I doubt it is a coincidence that the date chosen for the probably fabricated Stranger's Visit allegory, 1794, is also the year that Thomas Paine's *The Age of Reason; Being an Investigation of True and Fabulous Theology* became a best-seller in America. [184] The book advocated for deism, rejected miracles, and heavily criticized institutionalized religion. Paine was particularly critical of Catholic dogma. He once said, "One good schoolmaster is of more use than a hundred priests.

Within the Wizard Clip story's construct, it is also worth noting that the religious advisors in the legend who failed to help the Livingston family held either British or German heritage, two of the initial cultures to embrace Protestantism. The inability of the Lutheran Church to combat the situation is a prominent theme throughout the story; however, the other denominations mentioned also had a contentious history with the Catholic Church. The first, Reverend Balmain, was Episcopalian. That organization split ties with the Church of England after the American Revolution but retained its Anglican doctrine. The Church of England renounced papal authority in 1534, only thirteen years after the Edict of Worms declared Martin Luther an obstinate heretic and banned the reading or possessing of his writings. Until the American Revolution, the Church of England was the official church of the Virginia colony.[185]

The second group of Protestants that tried and failed to help was Methodists. Methodism began as an internal reform movement within the Church of England led by British theologians John and Charles Wesley, and the undertaking led to the founding of the Methodist Episcopal Church in 1784 in America.[186] Interestingly, the Wesley brothers sought to reduce the Calvinist influence on the church, and their camp revivals helped spawn the First and Second Great Awakening, the latter of which was ongoing during the Wizard Clip events. The Second Great Awakening in North America revived supernatural belief among evangelical Protestants, as it rejected the skepticism, deism, Unitarianism, and rationalism left over from the American Enlightenment.[187] Reverend Gallitzin's remark that the Methodists attempting to help the Livingston family "began to pray and bawl" could be a slight toward the fiery, emotional method of ministering associated with evangelicals of the time.

The Wesley family claimed to suffer through a famous poltergeist-like event from December 25, 1716, through January 1717, the Epworth Rectory Haunting.[188] However, it is unclear if this affair motivated the brothers to rethink Reformed principles such as the doctrine for the cessation of miracles. Nevertheless, John Wesley notably complained about the English relegating witchcraft and apparitions to "old wives' tales" because, to him, that belief system contradicted the Bible.[189]

COMPETITION WITH SPIRITUALISM

The initial waves of Catholic nostalgia regarding the Wizard Clip legend coincided with the apex of two distinct periods of spiritual upheaval in America. Joseph Mobberly and Reverend Mulledy's curiosity about the Wizard Clip legend aligned with a peak of religious fervor during the Second Great Awakening, a movement that gave rise to new competing Christian denominations like Methodists and Latter-day Saints. It is unclear if the massive Protestant revival motivated these men to research a supernatural Catholic conversion story; however, the reasons for several Catholic priests to retell the story later in the nineteenth century is evident: belief in Spiritualism. Revered Finotti's interest in the legend in the 1870s aligns with Spiritualism's height of popularity. He noted plainly in his 1879 monograph that he could quickly cash in on the craze if it weren't for his scruples:

Surely, I have the whole army of Spiritists at my back. For although I readily admit that there may be truth in Spiritualism, I can (and the reader will agree with me) appeal to the very best of historical authority for facts parallel in their nature and development to those averred in Cliptown without being under any obligation to modern Spiritism, which is not of God.[190]

After attempting to distance himself from Spiritualists, Finotti later explained that his belief in the Wizard Clip haunting is well grounded in the scruples of the many good men and women of both Catholic and Protestant faith who provided similar firsthand testimony. He argued that "there is prima facie evidence in these pages, which carries conviction in its words" and that individuals who refused to admit that the manifestation affected them were "of doubtful character." Before asking the reader to consume his evidence and "judge for thyself," Finotti claimed that he sought opposing viewpoints but could find none except "some slight cynicism or stupid doubt."[191]

Reverend Finotti's description of the doubters is somewhat hypocritical on at least one occasion. He claimed to have talked with Richard McSherry, MD, in the same manuscript. Dr. McSherry was the eldest child of Richard and Anastasia McSherry. After describing Dr. McSherry as "a venerable man, a justly-trusted physician, and a highly revered citizen," Reverend Finotti recorded how Dr. McSherry claimed that his father, Richard, had no direct knowledge of the Wizard Clip events. During this conversation with Father Finotti, Dr. McSherry stated that he was born in 1792 and remembered the "Prince Missionary's" visit of several weeks' duration "to gather facts about Livingston and his family—but his father knew none except hearsay and tradition."[192]

It is notable that Dr. McSherry and his sisters have differing opinions about the truth of the manifestations. Another sibling, James McSherry, asked to review Reverend Finotti's finished product before publication because "there were some papers published a few years since in the *Baltimore Mirror* which were not authorized by our family and which did not please us."[193] James McSherry was born in 1807, studied law at Georgetown, and became a prominent lawyer. Perhaps the brothers' respected professions necessitated disavowing their belief in the ghost story.

A Catholic newspaper, the *St. Louis Leader*, first published the story referenced by James McSherry in December 1855; it was reprinted the following January in newspapers across the country, including a Baltimore newspaper called the *Catholic Mirror*. This periodical is most likely the one

James referenced as the *"Baltimore Mirror,"* and its editors published an updated version in May 1860. According to the 1860 edition titled "A True Ghost Story: The Cliptown Spirit," the 1856 account comprised:

1. A statement made by Dr. J.V. Huntington, the editor of the *St. Louis Leader*, about what he heard from reputable sources.
2. Two letters from Reverend Gallitzin, which are almost certainly the same two that he wrote to Catherine Doll (daughter of Anastasia McSherry).
3. Anastasia McSherry's two letters written to her brother about the experience.[194]

The 1860 account retains and elaborates on most of the story's earlier key points. The main difference is that this version includes "a statement made by Mrs. Anastasia McSherry to her children at Retirement Farm, Jefferson Co., Virginia respecting the strange things that happened to Mr. Livingston, which was heard and written down by one of her daughters." This revised oral history emphasizes her family's involvement in the happenings. It is uncertain if James McSherry objected to the entirety of this article or only the new information added since the *Catholic Mirror* first reprinted Dr. Huntington's story in January 1856, but it appears to be the latter. The article's author, the *Catholic Mirror*'s chief editor, Reverend Louis Obermeyer, noted that he needed to update the 1856 article for two reasons. First, the *Catholic Mirror* obtained new information from a surviving family member of Mrs. McSherry. Secondly, like Reverend Finotti, Obermeyer was motivated to use the story to criticize Spiritualism. Reverend Obermeyer claimed, "We feel confident all will take a deep interest in this narrative of an event which at the time of its occurrence was the wonder of the day, though since that the Satanic operations of Spiritism have somewhat familiarized us with preternatural doings."[195]

Other Catholic newspapers were making similar claims. For example, in January 1856, the *Boston Pilot* reprinted the *St. Louis Leader*'s article on the Wizard Clip, attaching another piece at the end "as a specimen of what modern spiritualists are doing."[196] The editor claimed that the report from a Spiritualist journal called the *North Western Orient* was evidence that "a vast diabolical development in this country is too clear to be doubted." The author questioned if Spiritualist communication with the dead was ushering in the Anti-Christ and denounced them as "miserable slaves of demons." The connection these Catholic periodicals were trying to make between

Spiritualism and the Wizard Clip legend seems to be twofold. First, belief in miracles and the real threat of supernatural attack are justified; second, Spiritualism is necromancy.

Reverend Obermeyer obtained the additional information for his 1860 article from the daughter of Dr. Huntington's source, Helen Nicholson. Mrs. Nicholson was the granddaughter of Anastasia McSherry. Helen's mother, born in 1804 and also named Anastasia but who went by Ann, likely penned the "statement" published in the *Catholic Mirror*. In a letter dated April 1, 1872, Helen further claimed that her mother furnished the "Clip papers" to Father Preston of Kentucky that eventually found their way into the *St. Louis Leader* in December 1855.[197] She recalled a somewhat conflicting version of the anecdote regarding the shirt with a burned handprint. Helen believed that someone gave a goatskin vest marked "I.H.S." by the spirit to the Conewago Church, and a red flannel shirt with a handprint burned into it was brought to a convent in Perry County, Missouri, by her aunt Susan Piet (McSherry) in 1840. She also claimed to have "known the lady well," meaning the Livingston girl whose thoughts caused the frightening encounter that resulted in the burned shirt, and they discussed the event often before she died in 1863. Reverend Finotti wrote to the school about the shirt and the fantastic story. Two retired nuns still lived at the convent and remembered Susan and her children but nothing about a burned shirt or the legend.[198]

Conversely, in a letter to Reverend Finotti, Susan Piet's son John Piet claimed to "have seen the old vest and handled it often" that "was cut all over in the shape of half-moons" before his mother gave it to the academy. John Piet, co-owner of Kelly, Piet and Company, published Reverend Finotti's book *The Mystery of the Wizard Clip*. In another letter obtained by Reverend Finotti, Susan's husband corroborated the details of the legend, stating that his wife talked so much about it that it became "a tiresome theme."[199]

Helen Nicholson told Reverend Finotti that she owned the cradle "by which the evil spirit rocked" her uncle William McSherry. She also possessed her grandmother's letters to her brother Samuel about the Voice at Livingston's, two letters from Reverend Gallitzin to her aunt Catherine Doll about the events, and, most curiously, "the crucifix from which our dear Lord spoke to my grandmother." She then illustrated how her grandmother's ghost foretold her mother's death:

> *My mother was often favored by supernatural visitations. She was told while kneeling at church to prepare and make her last confession. She did so, told the*

Father confessor of it, then she came home to my house and gave the children her last farewell. She then made all her last arrangements, how she was to be buried, etc. That same evening, she was taken ill and died on the third day from the warning (which had been given to her by her own mother).[200]

In another letter dated April 22, 1872, Helen elaborated on this story that first appears in Joseph Mobberly's 1825 Livingston's Conversion, which she called the "Georgetown record."[201] In Mobberly's account, Anastasia stayed home with a sick child while the rest went to church. As she began to pray, a beautiful person appeared in a light cloud with one hand up and another down, with a nail running through each. The man said, "Whatever you do for one of my little ones, you do for me." Anastasia kept the visit to herself until the Voice revealed the event's details to Adam Livingston.[202] Helen used this story to explain why her grandmother's ghost warned her mother of her impending death:

When as you will see in your Georgetown record, Grandma was praying before her crucifix. It was on Holy Thursday—her custom was to go to Frederick every Holy Week to attend the services—this time, her babe was sick—my mother was the babe—the voice which spoke to her from the crucifix made her raise her eyes, and told her "That child would comfort her yet." So, it proved for when grandmother was dying; she left her youngest child, then about one year old, to my mother's care and made her promise that if she would do a mother's part to the babe, she, Grandma, would ask Almighty God to grant her whatever she most wished. My mother asked to know of her death when it was near, and grandmother promised to give her three days' notice, which she did, and my mother faithfully did her duty to her little sister.[203]

It is unclear when Ann wrote Anastasia's "statement" or why Ann's daughter, Helen, modified the story about her grandmother's miraculous visit. Anastasia McSherry died a little over two years after her husband on December 4, 1824. Her daughter Ann was twenty and unmarried. Ann and two younger sisters, Catherine (age fourteen) and Cecelia (age eight), likely lived with Anastasia when she died. Their seventeen-year-old brother, James, was probably attending Georgetown but may still have lived at home. According to the *History of the Lower Shenandoah Valley Counties of Frederick, Berkeley, Jefferson, and Clarke*, Anastasia and Richard had nine children. Still, it names only eight of them, so Helen's claim is possible but highly unlikely, considering Anastasia would have birthed the baby in her early fifties, and Richard died more than two years before his wife. Nonetheless, Ann probably cared for the remaining children in the house after her mother's death.

Regardless of problematic details that are bound to form in any tale over time, it is evident that several female McSherry family members had good reason to believe the crux of the Wizard Clip story to be true. Anastasia's account seems partially corroborated by Father Gallitzin's letters to her daughter Catherine in 1839 and Mary Livingston's 1798 letter to the *Potomak Guardian*. Reverend Finotti and other Catholic authors believed the story was true, irrespective of their motivations for retelling it. Furthermore, several witnesses allegedly observed strange evidence of the haunting at a church in Conewago before Reverend Lekeu destroyed it in 1830.

Conversely, at least two of Anastasia's sons wanted to distance themselves from the legend, even claiming that their father knew nothing about the odd happening at Adam Livingston's home except for hearsay. Reverend Phelan believed that the affair was a hoax in 1798. The retired nuns who taught at the convent-run academy when Susan Piet's (McSherry) children attended could not remember anything about a miraculously burned shirt Susan left in 1840. Finally, the *History of the Lower Shenandoah Valley Counties of Frederick, Berkeley, Jefferson, and Clarke*, which provides a detailed genealogy of the McSherrys, prefaces the section on Middleway as a town noted far and wide for the spot where the famous operations of clipping spooks occurred. It avows that the event is "doubtless a clever piece of hocus-pocus on the part of somebody who wanted to get some property at a low figure."[204]

While we do not know their motivation, it seems clear that Anastasia McSherry and many of her female descendants are the chief suppliers of Wizard Clip legend elements. Until Father Gallitzin's first account turns up, the oldest comprehensive record allegedly derives from an interview of Anastasia McSherry by two Catholic priests in 1817, copied and preserved for Georgetown College by Joseph Mobberly in 1825. Some details are available in two letters Anastasia wrote to her brother while the events were occurring, Reverend Gallitzin's 1820 *Letter to a Protestant Clergyman* and his two letters written in response to Anastasia's daughter Catherine's inquiries about the haunting. Reverend Gallitzin wrote the letters to Catherine Doll in 1839, fifteen years after Anastasia's death. The most detail comes from Anastasia's "statement," written by her daughter Ann with some details elaborated on later by Ann's daughter Helen in letters to Reverend Finotti in 1872. Anastasia's statement is undated, but as Ann was the source of the data used in the *St. Louis Leader*'s 1855 article about the Wizard Clip, it is safe to assume that she hadn't written it yet. The statement appeared in the *Catholic Mirror* in 1860, and Ann died in 1867.

We will never know the full facts of what occurred in that tiny hamlet near the Potomac. If the whole affair was merely a confidence scheme by the Catholic Church, why did the organization abandon the property for more than 120 years after Adam donated it? Conversely, if the Catholic exorcism worked, why did Reverend Phelan reinvestigate the alleged haunting a year later? Why didn't Adam or any of his children write about it, or Father Cahill, for that matter? What role did Mr. Gorman play? The inability to find specific answers to these questions is frustrating, but looking at similar folklore provides another possible reason for some of the story's details: migration.

THE DEVIL OF GLENLUCE

Beliefs and traditions as part of a culture drift along with the migration of groups, often adapting to new environmental stimuli as they travel. We've established that Adam Livingston's family immigrated to America to avoid continued religious persecution by Catholic sovereigns, and his cultural group likely held genuine fear of witchcraft and preternatural attack. However, the Wizard Clip plot primarily stems from the wealthy, educated Irish Catholic McSherry family.

Richard McSherry grew up in St. John's Point, Ireland, less than seventy-five miles as the crow flies across the narrow North Channel from Glenluce, Scotland. Anastasia descended from English immigrants. While there is no direct evidence that the McSherrys knew of a story from Scotland called the Devil of Glenluce, similarities between it and the Wizard Clip are uncanny. Whether he or his wife knew of the tale is impossible to prove. Still, it is likely due to Richard's hometown proximity alone and the Scotch-Irish community they were a part of in America.

The story became popular after a widely distributed English book on demonology included it. King James's *Daemonologie* paved the way for many similar works attempting to prove the existence of the preternatural throughout the seventeenth century. Many of these authors were well-educated authorities in their field, lending legitimacy to the European witch hunts. Examples include Joseph Glanvil's 1681 publication *Saducismus Triumphatus: Or Full and Plain Evidence Concerning Witches and Apparitions*; Richard Bovet's 1684 *Pandemonium or the Devil's Cloyster: Proving the Existence of*

"Devil of Glenluce." *Lucy Elliot.*

Witches and Spirits; and Cotton Mather's 1693 *The Wonders of the Invisible World: Observations as Well Historical as Theological, upon the Nature, the Number, and the Operations of the Devils.* In 1685, Scottish mathematician and engineer George Sinclair included the Devil of Glenluce story in his immoderately titled book *Satan's Invisible World Discovered: Or a Choice Collection of Modern Relations, Proving Evidently Against the Atheists of This Present Age that There Are Devils, Spirits, Witches, and Apparitions, From Authentic Records and the Attestations of Witnesses of Undoubted Veracity: To Which is Added, the Marvelous History of Major Weir and His Sister, the Witches of Bargarran, Pittenweem, Calder, Etc.*[205]

Sinclair, a professor at the University of Glasgow, claimed secondhand knowledge of this event. He learned it directly from a student who professed to be a victim. He described it as "a true and short account of the trouble wherewith the family of one Gilbert Campbell, by profession, a weaver, in the old parish of Glenluce in Galloway, was exercised [*sic*]." The student, Gilbert Campbell's son, claimed that it began in October 1654 after a beggar named Alexander Agnew threatened to hurt his family because they denied him alms.[206] Authorities hanged Agnew three years later for blasphemy. Professor Sinclair implied that Agnew conjured a spirit to torment the family. True to his reformed belief system as a Presbyterian in the 1600s, Mr. Sinclair never described the spirit as a ghost. In the tale, the entity is called the voice, the spirit, the devil, the demon, the foul fiend, the foul thief, and even Satan.

The haunting began as a random shrill whistling in and outside the house. According to witnesses, the sound was similar to the resonance made by toy glass whistles. One afternoon, one of the daughters, Janet Campbell, became annoyed by the whistling as she left home to get a bucket of water and complained under her breath, "I would fain hear thee speak as well as whistle."[207] "I'll cast thee, Janet, into the well," a threatening voice unexpectedly replied. This sudden manifestation was extra disturbing because it was a perfect mimic of Janet's voice.

Around mid-November, the entity began throwing stones at the house's doors and windows and occasionally down the chimney. Poltergeist-like events grew with time. One evening, the family returned home to find all their trunks open, with the contents tossed about the house. That night, the spirit pulled blankets off family members while they slept and began taking their things and hiding them. It woke them almost every night. The family tolerated these childish annoyances until a particularly bothersome morning when Gilbert found his "warp and threads cut as if by a pair of scissors," hindering his work and angering him intensely. Gilbert's reaction opened a torrent of clipping. The spirit clipped coats, bonnets, hose, and shoes, often while being worn by a family member. Gilbert could not work, as it destroyed each weaving project he undertook.

After suffering secretly for weeks, Gilbert revealed his family's dilemma to a minister of his Presbyterian parish and his neighbors. A neighbor advised that he send his children away to see if the activity would cease, and it did. Nothing happened in the home for five days, after which Gilbert's minister insisted that the children return home and that Gilbert and his wife perform their parental duties. The house remained quiet until Thomas returned the following Saturday. The next day, something set fire to the house, but neighbors returning from church put it out without much damage. It was set ablaze again on Tuesday morning, being saved once more by the swift action of a neighbor.

Convinced that Thomas was either the problem or the focus of the spirit's ire, Gilbert asked his minister to keep the boy. The minister consented but assured Gilbert that Thomas was not the problem and was proven right as the paranormal activity intensified the first night Thomas was away. The remaining family members were pricked awake by pins and violent attacks on the house. Parts of the roof and walls were broken off and thrown at them throughout the evening. The next day, Gilbert sent for the minister and Thomas. As the boy entered the property, a sinister voice forbade him from entering the home. Ignoring it, Thomas crossed the home's threshold only to be assaulted so savagely that the minister promptly escorted him back to his house.

On Monday, February 12, the entire family began to hear the voice. It kept them up until midnight, asking and answering questions. The conversation and acknowledgement must have pleased the spirit, as it finally let them rest. Hearing this, the minister returned with some trusted parishioners. As they entered the home, the entity loudly exclaimed, "A dog!" Thinking that to be an insult, the minister rebuked the demon, only to be informed by it, "It was not to you, sir, that I spoke. I meant the dog over there." A hound had wandered in through the open door behind them.

The group began to pray, attempting to rid the house of evil. A voice under one of the beds interrupted them, asking, "Would you know the Witches of Glenluce?" It named five women, but Gilbert said this accusation was untrue as one was long dead. The spirit replied, "It is true, she died long ago, but her spirit is living with us in this world." Determined to exorcise the home, the minister returned the following day with Tom. The demon shrieked and warned that if Thomas didn't leave, he would set fire to the house again. The minister retorted that God would not permit it and "shall remove thee in due time." The devil countered that he would outlast the minister. This prediction proved accurate, as the minister died in December 1655.

One evening, after much frustration, the minister demanded to know from where the spirit came. An arm appeared in the center of the room and began beating on the floor so powerfully that it shook the entire house. It roared, "Come up, father, come up! I will send my father among you." Terrified, Gilbert cried out for the spirit to show itself. The entity menacingly dared Mr. Campbell to put out the candles, and it would come to the house "among you like fireballs. I shall let you see me indeed!" The petrified men did not blow out the candles.

The spirit continued to accuse villagers of witchcraft. It claimed that Robert Hay, a man the party knew to be honest and good, was a warlock. Then when the men failed to act on this accusation, the spirit appeared to mock them for the credulity of the ongoing European witch hunts. It loudly proclaimed, "A witch, a witch, there is a witch sitting upon the roost; take her away!" It was referring to a hen.

The minister tried and failed to exorcise the Campbell home for the rest of his life. He and the entity would engage in a religious debate after the minister's unsuccessful prayers almost every night for several months. Changing tactics, the minister ordered all to ignore the devil, which worsened the trouble. It began striking everyone in the house and throwing stones at anyone who came close to the home. It destroyed all of their food and shattered their dishes against the walls. Its anger grew, and it began screaming and cursing relentlessly; it threatened to burn the barn and home if no one would give it attention. The paranormal activity culminated around September 18, 1656, with four nights of fires that emanated from the family beds as they tried to sleep.

Mr. Sinclair abruptly ended the story at this unsatisfying point. He concluded, "The good man lived several years after this in the same house, and it seems by some conjuration or another, the devil suffered himself to be put away and gave the weaver a peaceable habitation. The weaver has been a very old man that endured so long these marvelous disturbances." Oddly, he did not attempt to tie the hanging of Agnew with the end of the Campbell haunting. It seemingly goes away on its own eventually, like the Wizard Clip Voice. We may never definitively prove that Wizard Clip chroniclers borrowed directly from this older folklore. However, many shared details of the two stories, such as the spontaneous combustion of family beds and clipping of objects, point in that direction.

The Bell Witch

The impetus of this entire project was my curiosity in exploring the similarities between the Bell Witch and Wizard Clip stories. They are too analogous to be a coincidence. I had not yet discovered the Devil of Glenluce legend when I contacted Heather Moser about the project. Heather is a classicist and a well-known authority on Appalachian folklore. She is the lead researcher for the Small Town Monsters production company, joining the team to work on its documentary *Mark of the Bell Witch*. I can't think of a better person to tell the Bell Witch tale. What follows is her take on arguably America's most famous ghost story:

> Over two hundred years ago, just south of the Kentucky border at the Red River settlement in Robertson County, Tennessee, the legend of the Bell Witch was born when a faceless entity began terrorizing the Bell family in 1817. Its malevolent behavior persisted through 1821, with activity reaching a fever pitch on the morning of December 20, 1820, when

John Bell, Sr.'s life ended abruptly. This story persists today in Adams, Tennessee, populated by just over 600 people. Children grow up hearing about the Bell Witch and the importance of not disrespecting her, even going so far as to elevate her to Bloody Mary–like status. Students dare each other to look into a mirror and say aloud, "I don't believe in the Bell Witch," three times on the off chance that she may appear. Locals are still known to blame any ill fortune on the Witch.

Ghost story, you may wonder, how could a tale of an entity called the Bell Witch fall into the realm of a specter? It is true from a folkloric aspect that the events recounted throughout history include elements typical of a witch tale.[208] However, ghost motifs are some of the central tenets for which the Bell Witch is most famous.[209] Perhaps the biggest argument for the Bell Witch being a poltergeist tale, above all else, is that the Witch herself was never actually seen, only heard, and her attacks were physically felt. Richard Williams Bell refers to the entity by many monikers: phenomenon, sounds, capers, witch, spirit, seer, and goblin, among others. The specter itself claimed to be many different things, leaving the Bell Family to speculate what exactly was plaguing their family and why. Popular opinions ranged from the entity being a disturbed Native American spirit to the ghost of an immigrant who left behind a buried treasure to an entity summoned by witchcraft or simply a spectacle created by the Bells for monetary gain.[210]

Regardless of what the entity claimed it was or popular opinion may be, the name "witch" has undoubtedly persisted in no small part due to the period in which this story takes place. Anything resembling any evildoing was witchcraft, and a story involving a murderous spirit fits the bill.

The general breakdown of the story goes as follows: John Bell Sr. and his family moved from North Carolina to Tennessee in the early 1800s. It did not take long before they were firmly established within their community. Records tell us that the family was well respected amongst their neighbors, and John Bell was important to the Red River Baptist Church as he was given the title of "Elder" within the community.[211] Despite their respected standing among their neighbors, an otherworldly creature chose to target the Bell Family for reasons that are still purely speculative.

It all began when John Bell, the Bell family's patriarch, inspected his crops. While in the field, he spotted a rather odd-looking creature with a dog's body and a rabbit's head. Startled by the vision before him, he shot at the animal, only for it to vanish before his eyes. It wasn't the only odd creature to suddenly appear on the farm. One of the Bell sons also

Heather Moser. *Provided by Heather Moser.*

witnessed an unnaturally large bird sitting on the fence post. In other words, strange happenings were beginning to occur on the property.

Shortly after the odd creatures were spotted, activity started within the home. At first, loud bangs were heard smacking off the side of the Bell cabin. Then the children could hear what sounded like rats gnawing on their bedposts, and their bedcovers would be constantly ripped from their beds. Of course, once the lamps were lit, nothing could be seen. Voices, which were at first indecipherable, were audible throughout the night.

John Bell's daughter, Betsy, was the first to face bodily harm. Without rhyme or reason, often her hair was pulled, her face slapped, and her body pricked by invisible needles, causing the young girl to scream out in pain. The attacks were so violent that she would have visible marks on her body. Eventually, the spirit shared its penchant for physical assault with John Bell, focusing primarily on those two Bells for the torture.[212]

The Bell family, exhausted from night after night of no sleep, called upon their family friend, a neighbor named James Johnston, to help discover what was happening and how to end it. James and his wife spent the night at the Bell home, only to be attacked in the same manner that had befallen poor Betsy and her father. James, in anger, demanded that the spirit declare its name and purpose. Although neither of those questions was ever directly answered by the spirit, the invocation was enough to cause the Witch to begin talking regularly and clearly for all to hear.

It did not take long before the Witch's presence became quite well-known in the region. Records indicate that people came from all over the world to have an experience with the Witch, and none left disappointed, with some being physically assaulted by an unseen force before they had a chance to exit the Bell home. The more popular her story became, the more tricks she would reveal to the increasing number of visitors and vagrants.

The Witch did not fail to impress. She flaunted her religious knowledge by engaging in conversations with conviction, citing any relevant Biblical passage to strengthen her argument. She exhibited a unique ability to be in multiple places at once. This ability was a talent she exemplified in a couple of ways. She would sometimes recite sermons held concurrently on different ends of the county. Not only did she emulate the speeches word-for-word, but she did so while perfectly mimicking the voices of the preachers. Her mimicry could span thousands of miles as well. In one instance, a traveler from England distinctly heard his parents' voices while sitting in the Bell home. John Bell confirmed that he, too, listened to their voices, leaving the Englishman baffled. Likewise, as he explained in an update via letter a couple of months later, his mother could simultaneously hear him, leaving

"Bedcovers." *Lucy Elliot.*

her to wonder who "Mr. Bell" was and what exactly her son was doing while on his trip to America.

General Andrew Jackson and his men are said to have had encounters with the Witch. On the journey to the Bell farm, Jackson's wagon became stuck. Perhaps in goodhearted jest, Jackson blamed the Witch for the difficulty. Upon acknowledging the spirit, however, a disembodied female voice took responsibility for the hardship, and the wagon returned to regular working order. Later that evening, one of Jackson's men brazenly claimed to be a witch hunter and dared the Witch to make herself known. Brandishing a gun loaded with a silver bullet, he attempted to shoot toward the disembodied voice. His gun would not work correctly, and he was summarily run out of the house while physically assaulted by this unseen force: Jackson and the rest of his men left by morning.[213]

Unfortunately, John Bell and some foolhardy visitors were not the only people plagued by the Bell Witch. As mentioned earlier, Betsy Bell was also a target. Indeed, it seemed that wherever Betsy went, tormenting followed. At one point, four distinct voices began speaking nightly; their presence is preceded by the scent of whisky in the air and culminates with nasty bickering, behaving much like a dysfunctional family. The voices had names and were heard by many, but they made themselves visible to Betsy one afternoon while she was visiting her sister in hopes of a few hours of reprieve. She was so frightened by their presence that she implored her brother-in-law to grab his shotgun. He could not see the entities but blindly shot into the orchard at Betsy's direction. This incident provided quite the conversational piece for the "witch family" that evening as they laughed about Betsy's unease and how one of them had a broken arm because of the blast.

Although the Witch delighted in physical and emotional attacks against Betsy, John Bell was the target of her most vile hatred. Over the years, he became very ill. It started with fits that rendered his tongue swollen, leaving him unable to speak or eat for hours and then for days. After suffering a seizure while surveying his fields with his sons, he became so weak that he could not leave his bed. The family summoned a physician to monitor his health, but one morning when they came in to check on him, he was unresponsive. John Bell, the patriarch of the family, had passed at some point during the night. A mysterious half-emptied jar sat beside his bed, which the family did not recognize. The only thing remaining in the vial was a bit of black liquid. Assuming that John had ingested whatever was in the jar and unsure of what the tonic contained, the eldest son took a drop *of it and gave it to the family cat, promptly killing the animal. The Witch's voice immediately proclaimed she gave John Bell a hefty dose of the liquid, which finally "fixed" him. She taunted her victory for days, even singing joyous exclamations at his funeral.*

Although the worst of the activity settled with the burial of John Bell, the Witch did appear a few more times to ensure that Betsy would not marry the love of her life, Joshua Gardner. Once their engagement was ruined, the Witch settled for seven years until her subsequent return. When she returned to the Bell family, she spent time with the eldest boy, John Bell Jr., and revealed prophecies of coming events. She disappeared after this, promising to return in 107 years.[214] It is unclear if she returned in 1935, but Charles Bailey Bell, a descendant of John, released a new book about the witch in 1933 in anticipation of her reappearance.

The Legend Returns

After the success of M.V. Ingram's 1894 book, *An Authenticated History of the Famous Bell Witch*, the folktale's popularity began to diminish.[215] By the twentieth century, the Bell Witch was arguably unknown to most outside Tennessee until *The Blair Witch Project* became a blockbuster in 1999. The film's plot involves a woman accused and convicted of witchcraft in Burkittsville (then Blair), Maryland, in 1785. She is cruelly sentenced to death by exposure and curses Blair's residents before perishing. Her ghost returns to exact revenge at various points in the future, either by bewitching others to do her bidding or killing the victims herself. The movie borrows elements from the Bell Witch legend, like murder and returning at various intervals that are decades apart. She terrorizes her victims first as a poltergeist whose powers become stronger with time. She can mimic voices, and only children can see her. The Wizard Clip story also may have influenced one of the movie's creators, Eduardo Sánchez. Mr. Sánchez grew up in Maryland and chose a place familiar to him as the setting for the film's plot. Burkittsville is twenty-five miles from Middleway, suggesting he likely knew about the legend.

The Bell Witch's popularity returned with a vengeance due to its association with *The Blair Witch Project*. Creators produced several films, hundreds of television shows, podcasts, and books about the Bell Witch since the movie's release. I do not know why the Bell Witch legend's fame continues to rise while the Wizard Clip remains relatively unknown in American pop culture. Both became popular initially through books released within fifteen years of each other during the height of Spiritualism.[216] If I had to guess, it is because of the heavy religious themes of Reverend Finotti's Wizard Clip story. Whereas M.V. Ingram's book about the Bell Witch reads like a novel, Reverend Finotti's manuscript is a poorly framed compilation of history and hearsay. Its ramshackle composition isn't easy to read, and the religious tone could be off-putting to some. Regardless, the Wizard Clip's place in history as a precursor to the success of these media ventures is evident.

ANALYSIS OF ALTERNATIVES

In my field, analysts sometimes come to me with a solution to a customer's intelligence requirement before ever performing structured thinking because it is faster and easier. Usually, this happens when the customer demands an answer to an intelligence question with an unreasonable deadline or the evidence points to a seemingly obvious solution. In either case, if overlooked, this is when intelligence failure can happen. When this occurs, I will assist the analyst in performing deliberate thinking by utilizing one or more structured analytic techniques to mitigate the risk.[217] These techniques help

Bell House, Middleway, West Virginia. *Author's collection.*

analysts challenge judgments, identify bias and manage uncertainty. Having said this, I admit that I fell into the very same cognitive trap at the onset of this project. I wanted to answer the question, "Why are elements of these three stories, which are unique in the pantheon of ghost legends, so similar?"

The parallels between the legends presented a seemingly obvious solution: folklore propagation due to migration. I became fixated on one specific detail in the Wizard Clip history, the sale of Adam Livingston's property to brothers Benjamin and Joseph Bell Jr. eight years before the Bell Witch haunting began. It seemed evident that these brothers were related to the Adams Tennessee Bells and that the story migrated with the family and adapted to its new Protestant environment. When Sharon Peery, a professional genealogist I hired, proved this untrue, I returned to the drawing board and performed an Analysis of Competing Hypotheses.[218] The three hypotheses I explored are familiar folklore propagation due to migration, the influence of religion on the mentally ill, and belief in legitimate phenomena absent the knowledge of similar recurring folklore.

With the help of Melissa Davies, a clinical psychologist, I eliminated mental illness as a viable hypothesis.[219] Hallucinations are a symptom of severe mental illness, which is debilitating without treatment. It is unlikely that Adam Livingston or others like him would be able to continue to work if that were the case. While manageable with modern medicines, this form of mental illness is incurable. It does not simply go away over time, leaving folklore propagation and belief in legitimate phenomena absent the knowledge of similar recurring folklore to explore further.

The precedent for elements of folklore to migrate is well established. Nearly every state in the union has a Lady in White ghost story. The Crybaby Bridge trope is so prolific that author James Willis catalogued more than thirty of these accounts in Ohio alone. Mr. Willis identified common ingredients of the stories, a bridge, a baby, someone to carry the baby onto the bridge (usually the baby's mother), and something that causes the baby to fall from the bridge. Likewise, the Devil of Glenluce, Bell Witch, and Wizard Clip legends contain three core narrative elements:

1. The haunting of an unsuspecting family begins small. Things go missing, and unexplained knocks and scratches start around the house, especially after dark. Sometimes family members begin seeing strange lights at some point, and the paranormal activity grows steadily in strength until full-on poltergeist phenomena commence.

2. Later, a voice appears with a highly developed understanding of Christian scripture.

3. These paranormal events last for years and end without explanation.

Plenty of other details in these stories suggest that elements of the legend traveled west from Scotland to Tennessee. Damage to property by fire and clipping is a common element of the Devil of Glenluce and Wizard Clip narratives, as are the protagonist's weaving skills. Distinct similarities between the Wizard Clip and Bell Witch stories include the entity tormenting men and children while having unexplained affection for a matriarch and its ability to bilocate. The Glenluce and Bell entities mimicked voices and seemingly needed the invitation to speak. All three spirits kept families sleep-deprived. Even small details like John Bell and Adam Livingston becoming overwhelmed by something mysterious while working their fields can suggest that Bell Witch storytellers appropriated elements from older folklore when crafting their narrative. Regardless of what raconteurs borrow and elaborate on, it does not rule out the possibility that something weird initiated belief in the legend.

As a realist, believing that for at least the past 369 years religiously dogmatic spirits occasionally materialize to terrorize unsuspecting families without reason is a tough pill to swallow. I have argued that there is no place for religion in my workplace because logical credibility is critical to the success of any intelligence analyst. Customers may not trust the arguments made in an intelligence assessment if they know that the author believes that a man parted a sea or another lived inside a whale for three days. Regardless of how I feel, belief in a legitimate recurring supernatural phenomenon presents a viable alternative to folklore propagation as a reason why eighteenth-century residents of Middleway feared the Wizard Clip entity.

Charles Bailey Bell's book *The Bell Witch: A Mysterious Spirit* never gained the popularity of M.V. Ingram's book.[220] Charles's work repeats Ingram's main themes and plotlines but significantly elaborates on the Witch's second visit in 1828. He claimed this is the reason he felt compelled to write the book. Charles, a physician, was John Bell's great-grandson. Like James McSherry's objection to the article "A True Ghost Story: The Cliptown Spirit," Charles professed that members of the Bell family protested vigorously against Ingram's publication. In the preface of his book, Charles stated, "The name Bell Witch has always been resented by the family. They are sensitive to such an appellation. The Bell Witch was not the old woman kind that was known so well in the East and Europe many years ago and, in many instances, burned at the stake. Neither was it the kind that could be punished in any way; with all its tangible actions, it had the faculty of vanishing instantly."[221]

Charles argued that the spirit was neither a witch nor a ghost. In my opinion, Charles's book describes the Bell entity as an eternal trickster akin to Pan or Loki. It claimed in its second visit to be millions of years old and said, "I am a Spirit from everywhere, Heaven, Hell, the earth; I am in the air, in houses, any place at any time."[222] Likewise, the Devil of Glenluce entity claimed that it was an evil eternal spirit sent from the bottomless pit of Hell to vex Gilbert Campbell's house and that Satan was its father.[223] The Voice of the Wizard Clip Legend claimed it was once flesh and blood and was suffering in Purgatory, but its inhuman powers could suggest otherwise.[224]

I'll admit that my biases hindered my objective thinking about this hypothesis. For weeks I struggled mightily to formulate a compelling argument. Then, one night in February 2022, it presented itself unexpectedly. I hit play on my podcast app and settled in for a night's rest. As I drifted off to sleep, Forrest Burgess read an e-mail that the *Astonishing Legends* crew had received the previous month.[225] I nearly fell out of bed as the e-mailer began to describe events that had an uncanny resemblance to the Wizard Clip.

Not every detail of his experience is comparable to Adam Livingston's, but the core precepts were unmistakable. The e-mailer prefaced his note by questioning if his experiences suggest he has bipolar disorder but later noted that his wife also witnessed some of the strange occurrences. He described how he was an "obnoxious and outspoken" atheist for thirty-two years but had undergone a life-altering series of paranormal events that led to his conversion to Christianity in October 2021. It began out of boredom during the first COVID-related lockdown in the United Kingdom, which started in March 2020. Curiosity about the paranormal, particularly extraterrestrials, led him to meditate on his garden deck between midnight and one o'clock in the morning every night. He would recite "mantras, invocations and invitations" and then sit silently and watch. He began to see what he initially thought were UFOs but then realized they were "just glowing orbs of light." One that hovered just above his house brightly shimmered and had a golden glisten, but "it did not project light."

He had to end these experiments abruptly after a week or two as poltergeist activity commenced in his home. Cupboards would pop open on their own. Glasses would fall off kitchen counters, and keys would go missing, appearing later in weird places. Then a series of "uniquely terrifying sleep paralysis encounters began." He did not describe these frightening encounters, but he claimed that they stopped when he began hearing a voice that would wake him, presumably from petrifying sleep paralysis. It continued to wake him at night, quoting Christian scripture. Both he and his wife began to have scripture read to them in their dreams by "disembodied voices and angelic figures." After this, answers to his prayers began materializing, leading to their conversion to Christianity.

This contemporary account hits on several essential elements of the comparable folklore I researched for this project. The principal difference between the e-mailer's tale and the Wizard Clip could be that storytellers have spent more than two hundred years elaborating on the latter. The e-mailer arguably partook in conjuring and witnessed an entity that emerged as a glowing light, only to be assaulted by a poltergeist and then saved by a voice that quoted Christian scripture after more than a year of strange and unexplainable events.

Either the e-mailer had extemporaneously read the same obscure folklore as I and used it to develop an analogous contemporary legend, or he believed his story to be true. If deception is not the motivation, then fear likely played a role in generating all of these legends, whether frightened by a hoax, a hallucination, or an actual occurrence misperceived or genuine. Pastor Matzke and the good people I met at Priest Field believe in the supernatural. When asked about the cause of spiritual interference, Pastor Matzke said, "In my experience, one portal opener would be the heavy use of drugs or alcohol. This substance abuse can facilitate a doorway because of the altered state of mind. Stress can be a factor, as well as intentionality. If you sincerely intend to contact something dark, you'll get something you likely haven't anticipated."

Alternatively, a skeptic will argue that I am still discounting my cognitive biases, particularly availability and confirmation bias.[226] The e-mailer converted to Christianity, not necessarily Catholicism, although he never mentioned the denomination to which he subscribed. As far as we know, no clergy became involved during the assault. The spiritual attacks he cited did not include clipping or spontaneous fires, and there were several other incongruences between his and the Wizard Clip story. However, what we believe about the authenticity of these events as a dissociated party does not matter. I do not believe in ghosts; however, my belief in this seemingly recurring phenomenon's legitimacy is immaterial and likely unhelpful to those who genuinely think that spirits have affected their lives.

Chapter 7

MIDDLEWAY TODAY

Τhe best part about taking on this project was making new friends in Middleway. The village immediately reminded me of home. I grew up in a onestop sign former coal mining company town along Little Beaver Creek called Negley, Ohio. With a population of less than four hundred, it's now primarily a bedroom community suffering severe economic decline. There is little commerce beyond an auto repair garage, a hardware store, and a convenience store. If you look closely, one can still distinguish the standardized coal mining company homes and the shell of its former company store, where employees used the company credit they received as wages instead of cash. The town shriveled after the company exhausted area coal deposits and moved on to better diggings.

Middleway has roughly the same population and is dealing with similar economic hardships. Still, its future is brighter thanks to community-wide interest in historical and folkloric conservation. The first time I pulled into Middleway, I was awestruck by the volume of preservation of early nineteenth-century architecture. Middleway is a time capsule. Clapboard homes adorned with distinctive nods to the legend, such as crescent moon–decorated chimneys, line the main street. There are no sidewalks or businesses. A guided tour eagerly provided by the hospitable local conservancy president, Jessie Norris, revealed churches and log cabin homes still pocked by errant musket shots from the Civil War Battle of Smithfield Crossing, lending a sense that the entire village is a functioning museum.

Above: Log home, Middleway, West Virginia. *Author's collection.*

Left: Chimney, Middleway, West Virginia. *Author's collection.*

Jessie's farm. *Author's collection.*

Jessie is the very embodiment of the quintessential small-town hostess. After several e-mail exchanges, she invited me to her roughly two-hundred-year-old home on Thanksgiving weekend. Formalities included meeting her amiable farm animals (which thankfully have all managed to keep their heads in place) and my new best friends, her dogs Findley and Rhett Butler. I am an introvert, but Jessie's hospitality quickly dissolved my anxiety about the meeting. I cannot imagine a better ambassador for this special place.

Jessie has a degree in early American history and is passionate about conserving Middleway's historical and legendary past. To her, they intertwine. She argues that the amount of verifiable historical data associated with Wizard Clip folklore makes separating fact from fiction difficult. She points to the Livingston land donation records still held at the county courthouse and Mary Livingston's unhappy letter to the editor of the *Potomak Guardian* newspaper as evidence that something strange and historic happened here more than two hundred years ago. Wizard Clip is Middleway history.

Jessie is proud that although the town is on the historic registry, the upkeep of the village is entirely volunteer based. There is no funding for preservation, and everyone does their best with what they have. She attributes much of the village's interest in conservation to the Wizard Clip legend. Jessie is enthusiastic about the recent upturn in interest that Middleway is enjoying

Legends & Lore Marker, Middleway, West Virginia. *Author's collection.*

and attributes at least some of it to the Pomeroy Foundation awarding her conservancy a West Virginia Folklife Program, Legends & Lore Roadside Marker Grant. This unique program promotes cultural tourism and commemorates legends and folklore as essential to every community's cultural heritage. Through the grant, the conservancy installed a metal road sign on Jessie's farm two years ago, resembling a historical marker, commemorating the Wizard Clip legend.

The Middleway Conservancy has no dedicated public meeting space and utilizes a shed to store its artifacts and records. A benefactor recently donated one of Middleway's many historic buildings to the organization. Used during the Civil War as a makeshift hospital, the organization hopes to acquire enough funds to renovate the building into a usable meeting and museum space. Jessie is hopeful that media exposure brought on by renewed interest in the legend will drive donations to this worthwhile cause.

PRIEST FIELD

Although the most damaging spiritual attacks have ended, reports of odd happenings persist at Priest Field. The founding director of the Priest Field Pastoral Center, Monsignor John L. O'Reilly, wrote in his 2001 book, *The Mystery of the Wizard Clip: Supernatural Visitations in Old Virginia and Their Remarkable Legacy*:

The strange phenomena that took place here so long ago still bring a sense of uneasiness to some. A local priest described a clammy feeling that would overcome him, compelling him to leave the property. He avoided the place except when the bishop came, fearing that his absence would be noticed.

On one occasion, a man and his wife came running out of the woods in a dither. The man held a camera and shook it in my presence, rattling as if the insides were loose. He said, "I was down at the Stranger's Grave and asked my wife to stand beside the cross, and the whole thing shattered in my hands when I lifted the camera to snap a picture."[227]

When I visited Priest Field in May 2022, a no-nonsense but warm and inviting facility manager named Susan Kersey, who lives on the property, described the continuing activity as not harmful or scary but mischievous. She has worked for the center for ten years and says that some employees are unnerved by the odd goings-on, but the majority laugh off strange occurrences by joking that the wizard is back. She noted that most examples are innocuous, like a critical document will occasionally go missing for more than a week, only to turn up exactly where it had been. However, she also recalls vividly one occasion when all the smoke alarms went off at three o'clock in the morning. While searching for the cause with a maintenance

Priest Field Pastoral Center entrance. *Author's collection.*

Stranger's Grave trail marker. *Author's collection.*

worker, they both distinctly heard footsteps on the floor above them. They were the only two people on the property then, and there was no apparent reason for the alarms to go off. She also quickly noted that the nearby St. Peter's Chapel in Harper's Ferry is more spiritually active, especially the rectory, where several diocese priests refuse to stay.

Susan then posited a potential reason for the continuing activity. She said an exorcist priest came from the archdiocese in Washington, D.C., and stayed at the center for about a week. After some investigation, he believes that because Priest Field caters to the needs of recovering addicts, the homeless, and abused women, the location is particularly active due to its troubled clients. He thinks that some people needing Priest Field care come to the facility already under attack by wicked spirits and that those spirits may linger afterward. I asked if anyone else had examined the property. Susan answered that several groups had sought permission to ghost hunt, and at least one television production company was among them, but they've politely declined every request. Without saying another word, her body language conveyed that this kind of attention would not benefit their mission. Besides, Priest Field's thirty-four acres comprise a small percentage of Adam Livingston's former farm, and Adam's house was not on the Catholic Church's current property.

Susan had to prepare for a wedding party needing to tour the grounds. As we were winding down our talk, Susan wanted to impart something to me before I left. She asked if I was Catholic, to which I replied honestly.

I am not religious. She leaned in and softly, almost nurturingly, said, "If you believe in good and evil, then evil is caused by something. You must be aware of spiritual warfare. I've learned through my work here that usually, the week before we hold a retreat for the troubled, some person involved will feel the need to open up to me about how badly their plans were unfolding." She often needs to reassure all involved that "the evil one does not want you here. He does not want you to come," implying that Priest Field is a place dedicated to fighting spiritual warfare, and they are winning most battles. Even now, editing this portion months later, I note the irony of my random Amazon music mix playing the Rolling Stones song "Sympathy for the Devil" in the background.

Somehow, Susan knew that I needed to hear this message right then and there. Early 2022 was a tough time. In March, our family lost my beloved father-in-law to rapid-onset dementia. The previous November, my stepmother succumbed to COVID-19, and my thirty-three-year-old stepbrother died from liver failure brought on by alcoholism. I was struggling but never mentioned it. She did not preach, simply inviting me to come as often as I needed to find peace in the beauty of the center and its surroundings.

Afterward, I took a long walk along Priest Field's splendid trail system, contemplating Susan's words. Soaking in the calm of nature along Opequon Creek, I became restored, albeit briefly. I will almost certainly continue to visit when in need of respite. I suggest that if given the opportunity, you do the same. That day, I learned that whether or not the Wizard Clip legend is rooted in truth is inconsequential. Priest Field is where people needing help can find it; that is all that matters.

Epilogue

HAUNTINGS, EXORCISM, AND MENTAL ILLNESS

Melissa Davies. *Provided by Melissa Davies.*

P astor Matzke's assertion that clergy should address the potential for mental illness as causation in cases like the Wizard Clip prompted a conversation with Melissa Davies. Melissa is a longtime practicing clinical psychologist. We became acquaintants through our mutual affection for legends, and I have been a past guest on her podcast, *Ohio Folklore*. She was kind enough to answer several questions.

What illnesses might cause auditory and visual hallucinations?

Visual and auditory hallucinations occur as a symptom of severe mental illness. They can be associated with schizophrenia, schizoaffective disorder, bipolar disorder, and unipolar depression. Schizophrenia, schizoaffective disorders, and bipolar disorder usually manifest in the late teens or early twenties. A person with a family history of such conditions is at higher risk of developing them. Hallucinations of this type do not happen in isolation; they happen concurrently with other symptoms, including disoriented thinking, delusions, disorganized speech/incoherence and flat or inappropriate affect. These conditions are chronic and not curable, but they are manageable today with medications and supportive therapies.

Persons suffering severe forms of major depression also suffer hallucinations, which only occur during a depressive episode. Major depression is episodic, meaning depression is known to come and go over periods of time. Notably, severe symptoms like hallucinations do not occur when the person is not actively depressed. Other common symptoms of major depression include suicidal thinking, hopelessness, fatigue, sleep and appetite disturbance, and feelings of worthlessness. Unlike schizophrenia, schizoaffective disorder, and bipolar disorder, a person can develop major depression at any time in life. All conditions are susceptible to life stressors, meaning that stressful life events are known to worsen symptoms. Major depression can often be treated effectively and overcome. However, some people do not respond well to medications and therapies and must learn to manage the condition long-term.

Is increased religious zeal a typical symptom among those affected by a mental illness?

Certain types of schizophrenia are prone to fantastic ways of thinking, some of which may be religious. For example, if someone with schizophrenia believes they have the power to raise people from the dead, they may point to Bible scriptures showing that Jesus did the same. In this way, scriptures can serve to validate or confirm that such things have happened before and can, unfortunately, deepen the person's delusions. It's also not uncommon for such people to believe they are some important religious figure (i.e., Christ reincarnated, et cetera). When they are a part of such religious communities, it's easy to see how religious teachings can reinforce their delusions.

It's important to distinguish zealotry from pathology, however. Fervent religious beliefs do not increase a person's chances of developing a major mental illness. It can just make those already prone to mental illness more entrenched in delusional thought processes. However, excessive adherence to religious dogma can be related to obsessive-compulsive disorder (OCD). OCD is an anxiety disorder that stems from the need for exactness and perfection when complying with a moralistic code. OCD is not associated with hallucinations, however.

What (if any) was the treatment for these symptoms in the 1790s?

Mental asylums in the Americas were first built in the mid-1700s. These precursors to the psychiatric hospital were little more than warehouses for those suffering major mental illness. Persons deemed "mad" could be sent to such facilities by family members who'd become overwhelmed with the responsibility of caring for them.

During the Age of Enlightenment, near the end of the eighteenth century, attitudes toward mental illness began to shift. Those with mental illness were treated with compassion and support for the first time. Some religious communities, like the Quakers, developed facilities that allowed such people to integrate into their communities. Patients were housed in tiny homes and provided interaction with others regularly. While some large asylums still existed, these smaller and more integrated approaches were considered state-of-the-art treatments at the time.

How are these patients treated today?

Patients who suffer from these conditions today are generally treated on an outpatient basis with a combination of medications (i.e., antipsychotics, mood stabilizers, antidepressants) and psychotherapy. Many patients need occasional hospitalization, especially if they face much stress or other unexpected life events. Also, many patients struggle to stay on the medications for a few reasons. This includes some side effects which can prove intolerable (i.e., excess weight gain, tardive dyskinesia, sexual dysfunction, et cetera). If a person unintentionally skips doses, that can trigger a psychotic episode. Once delusions retake hold, it can be very difficult to convince the person they need to resume taking the medication.

We no longer use asylums for treatment. However, some rehabilitative facilities now serve people suffering from major mental illnesses. These are more like assisted living facilities for mental health patients; group homes are another format that works well for some people.

What is the likelihood that mental illness is the primary cause of alleged strange occurrences and disembodied voices described in the Wizard Clip legend?

Hallucinations are not specific but pervasive. The affected person experiences visual and auditory hallucinations in various settings, and mental illness is not situation specific. The person doesn't only experience hallucinations in one place. Therefore, if Adam Livingston were only known to have these experiences in one place, that would not indicate severe mental illness.

Hallucinations due to mental illness can and do change. New ones can pop up, and old ones can morph into something new. Some people compare it to the sensation of dreaming while you're awake. When you think of how bizarre dreams can be, you can imagine how various hallucinations can be. The more overriding feature of hallucinations (and any psychotic symptom) is their pervasiveness, meaning they occur in all settings. They are also lifelong (without treatment) and debilitating.

From what you've described of the Wizard Clip, it's unlikely that Adam Livingston's unusual experiences stemmed from mental illness. As I mentioned, hallucinations don't materialize outside of other symptoms (i.e., delusions, disordered thinking, flat affect, depressed mood, et cetera). People don't just experience hallucinations singularly (except for the abuse of hallucinogenic drugs, of course). Without effective treatment, those with severe mental illness cannot function independently (i.e., maintain employment, relationships, et cetera). Most cannot care for themselves on a daily basis. From what I understand, this does not seem to match up with the descriptions of Adam Livingston. I suspect that the church seized upon this tale as a mechanism to promote their teachings and encourage obedience among the laity.

From a medical perspective, are exorcisms necessary (whether there is a genuine need or a beneficial placebo effect), and if so, how might they be determined to be required?

Spiritual practices of all sorts, including exorcisms, can be of great benefit and value. Considering a person's cultural and religious background, they can offer insights into solutions that aren't offered by the secular world. On a separate note, the placebo effect is real and powerful. So, whether actual angels and demons are battling over a person's soul or the belief that such a battle is happening ends up helping the person resolve their dilemmas, we should be open-minded to the process.

When other "scientific" approaches have been exhausted, I think it's reasonable to consider solutions of the spiritual realm. Again, it's always important to consider each person's cultural background and values; any approach should align with those values. I'm not aware of any cases where exorcisms have caused harm, although I know horror movies love to portray dramatic and gruesome scenes. I am biased in believing that psychotherapy can benefit almost everyone, whether a person is battling demons or not. I would recommend it to anyone facing a life dilemma that feels overwhelming.

How does your mental health expertise influence your interest in folklore as a podcaster and author, particularly concerning research?

I appreciate this question and how it pulls my passions into one response! Over my seventeen years of independent practice as a clinical psychologist, I've heard countless stories from patients about their unexplained experiences. To be clear, the vast majority of my patients suffer mild to moderate depression and anxiety, not the severe illnesses I described earlier. These very sane people report discovering things like a recently deceased loved one's photograph somehow removed from the wall and placed in the center of a room, disembodied sounds, and crackling phone messages left by phone numbers that once belonged to their deceased loved ones.

In short, I've come to realize that there are some things about the way this universe works that we don't fully know or understand. And perhaps we're not meant to. Folklore is born of what remains in the gap between what we can explain and what we experience. Mystic experiences capture our imaginations. Because, as humans, we are meaning-makers, we draw upon our cultural backgrounds to tell a story to make it make sense. For many of us, that means turning to things like religious texts and oral histories, and this certainly seems to be the case with the Wizard Clip.

NOTES

Introduction

1. Swetnam, *Devils, Ghosts, and Witches*.
2. Clark, *Thinking with Demons*.

Chapter 1

3. To avoid confusion with another town in Virginia called Smithfield, residents changed the name of the village to Middleway in 1807. Jefferson County became part of West Virginia during the Civil War through annexation in 1863.
4. Bates, *Legend of Wizard Clip*.
5. Ryan, "Story of the 'Wizard Clip' or 'Clip Ghost.'"

Chapter 2

6. Finotti, *Mystery of the Wizard Clip*.
7. Brown, *Mystery of the Wizard Clip*.
8. Marshall, *Adam Livingston*.
9. Brown and O'Reilly, *Mystery of the Wizard Clip*.
10. Finotti, *Mystery of the Wizard Clip*.
11. Martin Luther's attempts at reform within the Catholic Church caused the schism that led to the Protestant movement and the Lutheran Church. French theologian John Calvin pushed for additional Christian reforms, resulting in Reformed denominations such as Presbyterians and Congregationalists.

12. Finotti, *Mystery of the Wizard Clip*.
13. Mobberly, *Livingston's Conversion*.
14. Finotti, *Mystery of the Wizard Clip*.
15. The Calvert family who established the colony of Maryland gifted the Jesuits the St. Inigoes tobacco plantation in 1637.
16. Marshall, *Adam Livingston*.
17. The Palatinate was a principality of the Holy Roman Empire situated along the Rhine River on the French border.
18. Cobb, *Story of the Palatines*.
19. Milnes, *Signs, Cures & Witchery*.
20. Napier, *Maleficium*.
21. Marshall, *Adam Livingston*.
22. Ibid.
23. Lancaster County was in the western portion of Pennsylvania's frontier at the time.
24. Ibid.
25. Ibid.
26. Doddridge, *Settlement and Indian Wars*.
27. Hintzen, *Border Wars of the Upper Ohio Valley*.
28. Hutson, *Religion and the Founding of the American Republic*.
29. Marshall, *Adam Livingston*.
30. Ibid.
31. Ibid.
32. Ibid.
33. Ibid.
34. Ibid.
35. *Catholic Mirror*, "Cliptown Spirit."
36. *Shepherdstown Register*, "Wizard Clip."
37. Finotti, *Mystery of the Wizard Clip*.
38. Ibid.
39. Ibid.
40. Ibid.
41. Finucane, *Ghosts*.
42. Marshall, *Adam Livingston*.
43. Finotti, *Mystery of the Wizard Clip*.
44. Barry, *Strange Story of Harper's Ferry*.
45. Finotti, *Mystery of the Wizard Clip*.
46. Norris, *History of the Lower Shenandoah Valley*.
47. Ibid.
48. Ibid.
49. Hutson, *Religion and the Founding of the American Republic*.
50. Ibid.
51. Marshall, *Adam Livingston*.
52. *Africa and the World*, "Christianity and Slavery."

53. Moscufo, "Churches Played an Active Role."
54. Finotti, *Mystery of the Wizard Clip.*
55. Green Thomas, "Georgetown Apologizes."
56. Brownstone, *Life of Demetrius Augustine Gallitzin.*
57. Ibid.
58. Ibid.
59. Ibid.
60. Ibid.
61. Ibid.
62. Mobberly, *Livingston's Conversion.*
63. Marshall, *Adam Livingston.*
64. Diocese of Altoona–Johnstown, "Servant of God Demetrius A. Gallitzin."
65. Finucane, *Ghosts.*
66. Ibid.
67. Ibid.
68. Jortner, *Blood from the Sky.*
69. Ibid.
70. Ibid.
71. Napier, *Maleficium.*
72. Hutson, *Religion and the Founding of the American Republic.*
73. A dog barking at the brother of Magistrate Dudley Bradstreet from nearby Andover was enough for a group of girls to accuse him of witchcraft. After issuing forty arrest warrants for those accused of witchcraft, Dudley refused to order more, resulting in sorcery accusations. Both men fled Andover until the craze was over; however, the dog was tried for witchcraft and hanged.
74. Napier, *Maleficium.*
75. Livingston, *Modern Christian Thought.*
76. The Second Great Awakening (1790–1840) was a religious revival in North America characterized by spiritual zeal, emotional outpouring and an appeal to the supernatural.
77. Weisberg, *Talking to the Dead.*
78. Brown, *Mystery of the Wizard Clip.*
79. Ibid.
80. Ibid.

Chapter 3

81. Finotti, *Mystery of the Wizard Clip.*
82. Mobberly, *Livingston's Conversion.*
83. Marshall, *Adam Livingston.*
84. Ibid.
85. Gilot, *Potomak Guardian,* August 29, September 12, 1798.
86. Finotti, *Mystery of the Wizard Clip.*

87. Marshall, *Adam Livingston.*
88. Finotti, *Mystery of the Wizard Clip.*
89. Ibid.
90. Ibid.
91. Barry, *Strange Story of Harper's Ferry.*
92. Chapter 1 briefly mentions this anecdote in Ryan, "Story of the 'Wizard Clip' or 'Clip Ghost.'"
93. *Wheeling Daily Intelligencer,* "West Virginia Ghost Stories."
94. Chapter 5 discusses the legend and its similarities to the Wizard Clip.
95. "McGinny" is almost certainly a misspelling of Minghini.
96. "I.H.S." is a Christian symbol and monogram for Jesus. It is an abbreviation for Jesus in Greek.
97. Finotti, *Mystery of the Wizard Clip.*
98. Ibid.
99. Ibid.
100. Ibid.
101. Ibid.
102. Marshall, *Adam Livingston.*
103. The portion of Reverend Gallitzin's letter referencing "old times" is quoted in Chapter 6.
104. Marshall, *Adam Livingston.*
105. Finotti, *Mystery of the Wizard Clip.*
106. Ibid.
107. Ibid.
108. Mobberly, *Livingston's Conversion.*
109. Finotti, *Mystery of the Wizard Clip.*
110. Mobberly, *Livingston's Conversion.*
111. In Mr. White's book *Witches of Pennsylvania,* he states, "Braucheri is usually translated as 'trying,' or sometimes 'using.' At the other end of the spectrum was Hexeri, or witchcraft."
112. In *Witches of Pennsylvania,* Mr. White describes witch bottles as "a charm to protect against or reverse the curse of a witch and possibly identify the individual responsible....Often witch bottles contained ritualized items representing the victim's pain or misfortune. They were mixed with the victim's urine and other bodily fluids and corked to trap the symptoms in the bottle and often reverse them on the witch."
113. Finotti, *Mystery of the Wizard Clip.*
114. Ibid.
115. Marshall, *Adam Livingston.*
116. Finotti, *Mystery of the Wizard Clip.*
117. Brownstone, *Life of Demetrius Augustine Gallitzin.*
118. Finotti, *Mystery of the Wizard Clip.*
119. Marshall, *Adam Livingston.*
120. Gilot, *Potomak Guardian,* August 29, September 12, 1798.

121. Reverend Finotti's book spells the name "Goreman," whereas it is "Gorman" in the older *Potomak Guardian* letters.
122. Marshall, *Adam Livingston*.
123. Ibid.

Chapter 4

124. Finotti, *Mystery of the Wizard Clip*.
125. Ibid.
126. Ibid.
127. Ibid.
128. Ibid.
129. Ibid.
130. Ibid.
131. Ibid.
132. Ibid.
133. Ibid.
134. Ibid.
135. Ibid.
136. Ibid.
137. Norris, *History of the Lower Shenandoah Valley*.
138. Finotti, *Mystery of the Wizard Clip*.
139. Ibid.
140. Ibid.
141. Ibid.
142. Napier, *Maleficium*.
143. Finotti, *Mystery of the Wizard Clip*.
144. Ibid.
145. Ibid.
146. Ibid.
147. Ibid.
148. Mobberly, *Livingston's Conversion*.
149. Finotti, *Mystery of the Wizard Clip*.
150. Brown, *Mystery of the Wizard Clip*.
151. Brown and O'Reilly, *Mystery of the Wizard Clip*.
152. Finotti, *Mystery of the Wizard Clip*.
153. Ibid.
154. Marshall, *Adam Livingston*.
155. Finotti, *Mystery of the Wizard Clip*.
156. *Richmond Enquirer*, "Virginia Legislature. House of Delegates."

Chapter 5

157. Milnes, *Signs, Cures & Witchery*.
158. Ophidiophobia is the irrational fear of snakes.
159. *Pebble Media*, "Baby Doll Dance in Lowellville, Ohio."
160. The early modern period of contemporary history spans roughly the years between AD 1400 and AD 1800.
161. Also known as the "Poor Men of Lyon," the Waldensians were a pre-Reformation Catholic congregation that rejected many of the church's principles, including belief in Purgatory.
162. Cawthorne, *Witches*.
163. Napier, *Maleficium*.
164. Ibid.
165. Ibid.
166. After witnessing a seemingly successful indigenous rain dance in 1612 near Jamestown, Reverend Alexander Whitaker wrote of the Powhatan Confederacy, "[T]here be great witches amongst them, and they are very familiar with the devil."
167. James R[X], *Daemonologie*.
168. Hudson, *Witchcraft in Colonial Virginia*.
169. Cawthorne, *Witches*.
170. Napier, *Maleficium*.
171. The Edict of Worms is a 1521 decree in which the Holy Roman emperor, Charles V, condemned Luther as "a notorious heretic" and banned citizens of the empire from propagating his ideas.
172. Cawthorne, *Witches*.
173. Ankerloo, Clark, and Monter, *Witchcraft and Magic in Europe*.
174. Livingston, *Modern Christian Thought*.
175. Ibid.
176. White, *Witches of Pennsylvania*.
177. Hudson, *Witchcraft in Colonial Virginia*.
178. Napier, *Maleficium*.
179. Ibid.
180. Jortner, *Blood from the Sky*.
181. Ibid.

Chapter 6

182. The Reign of Terror was a period of the French Revolution when revolutionaries confiscated church lands and priests were either killed or exiled. The new French Republic banned Catholicism in 1792 and briefly converted its churches, including Notre Dame, into Temples of Reason.
183. Gallitzin, *Defence of Catholic Principles*.
184. Paine, *Age of Reason*.

185. Hutson, *Religion and the Founding of the American Republic.*
186. Ibid.
187. Jortner, *Blood from the Sky.*
188. Finucane, *Ghosts.*
189. Jortner, *Blood from the Sky.*
190. Finotti, *Mystery of the Wizard Clip.*
191. Ibid.
192. Ibid.
193. Ibid.
194. Ibid.
195. Ibid.
196. *Boston Pilot,* "Ghost of Wizard Clip."
197. Finotti, *Mystery of the Wizard Clip.*
198. Ibid.
199. Ibid.
200. Ibid.
201. Ibid.
202. Mobberly, *Livingston's Conversion.*
203. Finotti, *Mystery of the Wizard Clip.*
204. Norris, *History of the Lower Shenandoah Valley.*
205. Sinclair, *Satan's Invisible World Discovered.*
206. Alms are gifts of money food or clothing to the impoverished.
207. Or, "I would rather hear you speak than whistle."
208. While reading accounts of the Bell Witch's antics in both M.V. Ingram and Charles Baily Bell (and any subsequent retellings of the tale), one can clearly see that the legend contains examples of the following folklore elements, which are outlined in the *Stith-Thompson Motif-Index of Folk-Literature.* There are more aspects not outlined within these notes, of course, but this is a decent sampling for our immediate needs: "Silver bullet protects against giants, ghosts, and witches"; "Magic knowledge of witches"; "Witches have power to see distant sights"; "Witch in form of dog"; "Witch in form of mythical animal"; "Witch in form of wild bird"; "Blue lights follow witches"; "Witch causes sickness"; "Witch cripples or lames through illness"; "Witch bewitches wagon"; and "Invisible witch sticks victim with pins."
209. Again, looking to the *Stith-Thompson Motif-Index of Folk-Literature* for examples: "Wagon refuses to move because ghost is sitting in it"; "Ghost chases pedestrian on road"; "Ghost pulls bedclothing from sleeper"; "Ghost disturbs sleeping person"; and "Ghosts frighten people (deliberately)."
210. The witch herself varied her answers as to what she was on multiple occasions, but she was consistent in her reasoning for the hauntings: to make John Bell's life miserable. It is also worth mentioning that, even to this day, she is often referred to as Kate because at one point she claimed to be a witch summoned by Kate Batts, a woman who was known in the area for her eccentric behavior.
211. This title and the ability to worship within the church were eventually taken away from John Bell, however, due to a dispute between John Bell and Benjamin

Batts that was eventually taken to criminal court. As Bell's charges spread bad publicity due to him being found guilty of "usury," the Red River Baptist Church ultimately excommunicated Bell in 1818. Despite attempts to be reinstated, John Bell was never able to be a member of the local church again.

212. Despite the physical attacks against John and Betsy, the witch did not treat everyone with such disdain. She had an affinity for John's wife, Lucy. She showed her affection by delivering food while she was ill and speaking kind and encouraging words to her throughout the entirety of this haunting.

213. Andrew Jackson later said that he would rather face the entire British army than deal with the Bell Witch.

214. During this time, the Bell Witch legend migrated to Mississippi when Betsy moved there after the death of her husband, Richard Powell. Today, that area has its own altered version of the Tennessee tale.

215. Ingram, *Authenticated History of the Famous Bell Witch*.

216. Finotti, *Mystery of the Wizard Clip*; Ingram, *Authenticated History of the Famous Bell Witch*.

217. For those interested in learning more about deliberate thinking, the author suggests Daniel Kahneman's *Thinking Fast and Slow* and Richards Heuer's *Psychology of Intelligence Analysis*.

218. While John Bell and Joseph Bell Jr. had family in Virginia simultaneously, Ms. Peery's research proved that these families are unrelated. The Scottish surname Bell is common, and the association of these two families to these two unique ghost stories appears to be a coincidence. Fun fact: The poltergeist that made Kate and Maggie Fox famous in 1848 claimed through table rapping to be a murdered peddler buried in their basement. When asked who committed the crime, the spirit responded, "John Bell." This John Bell previously resided at the house but found the accusations ridiculous. Groundwater thwarted attempts to discover the peddler's body.

219. See the epilogue for further details.

220. Bell, *Bell Witch*.

221. Ibid.

222. Ibid.

223. Sinclair, *Satan's Invisible World Discovered*.

224. Finotti, *Mystery of the Wizard Clip*.

225. *Astonishing Legends*, "Astonishing Junk Drawer #001," February 5, 2022.

226. Availability bias refers to the tendency to use the information we can quickly recall when evaluating a topic or idea, even if this information is not the best representation. Confirmation bias refers to the tendency to seek out information that supports something you already believe.

Chapter 7

227. Brown and O'Reilly, *Mystery of the Wizard Clip*.

BIBLIOGRAPHY

Archival Materials

Gilot, Jon-Erik. *Gallitzin Letters (1839).* Diocese of Wheeling–Charleston Archives, e-mail correspondence, August 2–3, 2021.

———. *Potomak Guardian*, August 29 and September 12, 1798. Diocese of Wheeling–Charleston Archives, e-mail correspondence, August 2–3, 2021.

Mobberly, Joseph P. *Livingston's Conversion.* S.J. Papers, Georgetown University Manuscripts, File—Box: 1, Folder: 1825.

Ryan, John J. "Our Scholasticate—An Account of Its Growth and History to the Opening of Woodstock, 1805–1869." *Woodstock Letters* 33 (1904). Woodstock College.

———. "The Story of the 'Wizard Clip' or 'Clip Ghost.'" *Woodstock Letters* 36 (1907). Woodstock College.

Articles

Africa and the World. "Christianity and Slavery: The Role of the Church." www.africaw.com.

Baltimore Sun. "Catholic Service Ends Contest Arising Over Haunted Farm." November 5, 1922.

Boston Pilot. "The Ghost of Wizard Clip, and a New Organ for Spiritualism." February 16, 1856.

Catholic Mirror. "The Cliptown Spirit." January 5, 1856.

———. "A True Ghost Story: The Cliptown Spirit." May 19, 1860.

Diocese of Altoona–Johnstown. "Servant of God Demetrius A. Gallitzin." www.dioceseaj.org/demetrius-gallitzin.

Downing, Bob. "Scaring the Devil: How They Exorcised the Wizard Clip." *Akron Beacon Journal*, October 26, 1980.

Gallitzin, Demetrius A. "A Defense of Catholic Principals." *Huntington Gazette*, 1816.

Green Thomas, Sandra. "Georgetown Apologizes for 1838 Sale of More than 270 Enslaved, Dedicates Buildings." *Georgetown University News*, April 18, 2017.

Meder, Theo. "The Talking Dead: Personal Communication with 'The Other Side' through the Ouija Board, Spirit of the Glass, and the Charlie Charlie Challenge." *Contemporary Legend*, series 3, volume 8 (2018).

Moscufo, Michela. "Churches Played an Active Role in Slavery and Segregation. Some Want to Make Amends." *NBCNews*, April 3, 2022.

New England Farmer. "The Tennessee Ghost." January 26, 1956. Reprint from the *Saturday Evening Post*.

O'Neill, Philip. "Reform Views of Purgatory." *Sunday Leader*, May 21, 1887.

Pebble Media. "The Baby Doll Dance in Lowellville, Ohio." July 18, 2019. https://pebble.media/news/fun/the-baby-doll-dance-in-lowellville-ohio.

Pennsylvania Gazette. "The Witch Trial at Mount Holly." October 22, 1730.

Richmond Enquirer. "Virginia Legislature. House of Delegates: Friday, January 7th Separate Elections." January 11, 1832.

Shepherdstown Register. "The Tale of Wizard Clip: A Wild Tale of Old Times in West Virginia." October 25, 1894.

———. "Wizard Clip." August 14, 1885.

Virginia Gazette. "Extract of a Letter About the Tryal of a Witch." January 13, 1737.

Wheeling Daily Intelligencer. "West Virginia Ghost Stories: Tales that Are Familiar in the Vicinity of Charlestown." March 12, 1891.

Books and Pamphlets

Ankerloo, Bengt, Stuart Clark, and William Monter. *Witchcraft and Magic in Europe*. Vol. 4, *The Period of the Witch Trials*. London: Athlone Press, 2002.

Barry, Joseph. *The Strange Story of Harper's Ferry: With Legends of the Surrounding Country*. Martinsburg, WV: Thompson Brothers, 1903.

Bates, R. Helen. *The Legend of Wizard Clip*. Middleway, WV: Press of Robert Smith, 1936.

Bell, Charles Bailey. *The Bell Witch: A Mysterious Spirit*. Nashville, TN: Lark Bindery, 1934.

Bond, Edward L. *Damned Souls in a Tobacco Colony: Religion in Seventeenth-Century Virginia*. Macon, GA: Mercer University Press, 2000.

Brown, Raphael. *The Mystery of the Wizard Clip: Diabolical Activity, Priestly Intervention, and Conversions in Colonial America*. Fitzwilliam, NH: Loretto Publications, 2010.

Brown, Raphael, and John L. O'Reilly. *The Mystery of the Wizard Clip: Supernatural Visitations in Old Virginia and Their Remarkable Legacy*. N.p.: Catholic Diocese of Wheeling-Charleston, 2001.

Brownstone, Sarah. *Life of Demetrius Augustine Gallitzin: Prince and Priest*. New York: FR Pustet & Company, 1873.

Brunvand, Jan Harold. *The Study of American Folklore: An Introduction.* New York: W.W. Norton & Company, 1978.

Cawthorne, Nigel. *Witches: The History of Persecution.* London: Arcturus Publishing, 2020.

Clark, Stuart. *Thinking with Demons: The Idea of Witchcraft in Early Modern Europe.* Oxford, UK: Oxford University Press, 1999.

Cobb, Stanford H. *The Story of the Palatines: An Episode in Colonial History.* New York: G.P. Putnam & Sons, 1897.

Doddridge, Joseph. *The Settlement and Indian Wars of the Western Parts of Virginia and Pennsylvania, 1763–1783.* Pittsburgh, PA: John S. Ritenour and William T. Lindsey, 1912.

Finotti, Joseph M. *The Mystery of the Wizard Clip.* Baltimore, MD: Kelly, Piet, and Company, 1879.

Finucane, Ronald C. *Ghosts: Appearances of the Dead & Cultural Transformation.* Buffalo, NY: Prometheus Books, 1996.

Gallitzin, Demetrius. *A Defence of Catholic Principles: In a Letter to a Protestant Clergyman to Which Is Added an Appeal to the Protestant Public.* New York: Catholic Publication Society, 1880.

Haughton, Brian. *Lore of the Ghost.* Franklin Lakes, NJ: New Page Books, 2009.

Hintzen, William. *The Border Wars of the Upper Ohio Valley (1769–1794).* Manchester, CT: Precision Shooting Inc., 1999.

Hudson, Carson O. *Witchcraft in Colonial Virginia.* Charleston, SC: The History Press, 2019.

Hutson, James H. *Religion and the Founding of the American Republic.* Washington, D.C.: Library of Congress, 1998.

Ingram, Martin V. *An Authenticated History of the Famous Bell Witch: The Wonder of the 19th Century, and Unexplained Phenomenon of the Christian Era.* Clarksville, TN: W.P. Titus, 1894.

James R[X] (James Charles Stuart IV). *Daemonologie.* N.p.: Robert Walde-Graue, Printer to the King's Majestie, 1597.

Jortner, Adam. *Blood from the Sky: Miracles and Politics in the Early American Republic.* Charlottesville, VA: University of Virginia Press, 2017.

Livingston, James C. *Modern Christian Thought.* Vol. 1, *The Enlightenment and the Nineteenth Century.* Upper Saddle River, NJ: Prentice Hall Inc., 1997.

Marshall, A.L. *Adam Livingston, the Wizard Clip, the Voice: An Historical Account.* Kearneysville, WV: Livingston Publications, 1978.

Miller, Harriet Parks. *The Bell Witch of Middle Tennessee.* Clarksville, TN: Leaf-Chronicle Publishing Company, 1930.

Milnes, Gerald C. *Signs, Cures & Witchery: German Appalachian Folklore.* Knoxville: University of Tennessee Press, 2007.

Musick, Ruth Ann. *The Telltale Lilac Bush and Other West Virginia Ghost Tales.* Lexington: University of Kentucky Press, 1965.

Napier, Gordon. *Maleficium: Witchcraft and Witch Hunting in the West.* Gloucestershire, UK: Amberley Publishing, 2017.

Norris, J.E. *History of the Lower Shenandoah Valley Counties of Frederick, Berkeley, Jefferson, and Clarke, Their Early Settlement and Progress to the Present Time; Geological Features; a Description of Their Historic and Interesting Localities; Cities, Towns, and Villages; Portraits of Some of the Prominent Men, and Biographies of Many of the Representative Citizens.* Chicago: A Warner and Company, 1890.

Paine, Thomas. *The Age of Reason; Being an Investigation of True and Fabulous Theology.* New York: G.P. Putnam's Sons, 1896.

Shea, John Gilmary. *History of the Catholic Church in the United States, 1783–1815.* Akron, OH: D.H. McBride & Company, 1888.

Sinclair, George. *Satan's Invisible World Discovered: Or a Choice Collection of Modern Relations, Proving Evidently Against the Atheists of This Present Age that There Are Devils, Spirits, Witches, and Apparitions, From Authentic Records and the Attestations of Witnesses of Undoubted Veracity: To Which Is Added, the Marvelous History of Major Weir and His Sister, the Witches of Bargarran, Pittenweem, Calder, Etc.* Reprint. London: Booksellers, 1814.

Swetnam, George. *Devils, Ghosts, and Witches: Occult Folklore of the Upper Ohio Valley.* Greensburg, PA: McDonald/Sward Publishing Company, 1988.

Taylor, James E. *The James E. Taylor Sketchbook: With Sheridan Up the Valley in 1864: Leaves from a Special Artist's Sketchbook and Diary.* Dayton, OH: Morningside House Inc., 1989.

Weisberg, Barbara. *Talking to the Dead: Kate and Maggie Fox and the Rise of Spiritualism.* San Francisco, CA: Harper San Francisco, 2004.

White, Thomas. *Witches of Pennsylvania: Occult History and Lore.* Charleston, SC: The History Press, 2013.

———. *The Witch of the Monongahela: Folk Magic in Early Western Pennsylvania.* Charleston, SC: The History Press, 2020.

INDEX

A

Adams, Tennessee 119, 125
Agnew, Alexander 115
Angel, the 27, 80
Augustine of Hippo 52

B

Balmain, Alexander 63, 68, 107
Barry, Joseph 36, 56
Bates, Helen 17
Batts, Kate 50
Bell, Benjamin 78
Bell, Betsy 120, 122
Bell, Charles 123, 126
Bell, John 119, 122, 126
Bell, John, Jr. 123
Bell, Joseph, Jr. 78, 125
Bell, Richard Williams 119
Bell Witch, the 104, 105, 118, 123, 126
bilocation 86
Blair Witch Project, The 123
Brown, Raphael 26, 52, 86
Brownstone, Sarah 71, 74

Burgess, Forrest 127
Burkittsville, Maryland 123

C

Cahill, Dennis 22, 46, 70, 75, 76, 80,
        89
Calvin, John 27, 92
Campbell, Gilbert 115, 116, 127
Campbell, Janet 116
Campbell, Thomas 116
Carpzov, Benedikt 92
Carroll, John 32, 38, 71
Catherine the Great 42
Catholic Mirror 109, 111
Cliptown 20, 56, 109
Cliptown Spirit, the 32, 110
Conewago, Pennsylvania 59, 71
conjurers 68, 70
Counterreformation, the 98

D

Daemonologie 94, 95, 96
Davies, Melissa 125, 137

Del Rio, Martin 92
Devil of Glenluce 114, 115, 127
Dickens, Charles 51
dreams 19, 21, 70, 128

E

Edict of Worms 98, 107
Enders, J. 60
Enlightenment, the 42, 50, 51, 63, 99,
    103, 106, 107, 139
Epworth Rectory Haunting 108
exorcism 14, 23, 46, 52, 65, 71, 72, 86,
    140

F

Farrell, Walter 52
Finotti, Joseph 16, 26, 32, 36, 74, 108,
    124
Fox, Kate and Maggie 51

G

Gallaher, John 89
Gallitzin, Demetrius Augustine 41, 46,
    58, 63, 71, 72, 106, 108
Gallitzin, Dimitri Alexievich 41
Germanus, Bishop 33
Gilot, Jon-Erik 37
Glenluce, Scotland 114, 115, 117
Gookman, Catherine 83
Gradual Abolition Act 31
Great Wagon Road 29, 62
Guy Fawkes Night 95

H

Hagerstown, Maryland 38, 55, 70, 74,
    88
Healy, James 80
Hesperius 52
Holy Roman Empire 98
Huntington, Jedediah 60, 65, 110

I

infestation 52, 67, 86
Ingram, Martin V. 123, 126
Inquisition, the 29, 92
Irving, Washington 51

J

Jackson, Andrew 122
Jefferson County, West Virginia 18,
    31, 89
Johnston, James 120

K

Kersey, Susan 133
King James 94, 96, 100
Kramer, Heinrich 92
Krauth, Charles 29

L

Liebenstein, Johann 29, 30, 59
Livingston, Adam 20, 31, 37, 39, 46,
    59, 60, 75, 80, 83, 134, 140
Livingston, Charlotte 83
Livingston, Eve 56, 87
Livingston, Mary Ann 31, 73, 79, 80,
    83, 88
Loretto, Pennsylvania 44
Luther, Martin 27, 47, 62, 92, 107

M

Malleus Maleficarum 92
Marshall, Anna 26, 29, 31, 34, 37, 54,
    61, 73
Mather, Cotton 95, 115
Matzke, Mark 62, 65, 128
Maximinus, Bishop 53
McClure, Dorothy 58
McSherry, Anastasia 27, 39, 79, 84,
    110, 112

McSherry, Ann 112, 114
McSherry, Dr. Richard 109
McSherry, James 109
McSherry, Richard 22, 38, 70, 76, 84, 114
McSherry, Rosa 56, 80
McSherry, William 41, 83
mental illness 63, 68, 125, 137
Middleway Conservancy 27, 132
Middleway, West Virginia 14, 17, 29, 30, 32, 34, 113, 129
Minghini, Joseph 22, 60, 76, 88
Mobberly, Joseph 27, 54, 59, 113
Moser, Heather 12, 118
Mr. Goreman 75
Mrs. Goreman 87
Mrs. Minghini 46, 88
Mrs. Spaulding 87

N

Nicholson, Helen 79, 88, 111, 112
Ninety-Five Theses 47
Norris, Jessie 129

O

Obermeyer, Louis 110
obsession 52, 86
O'Connell, Denis 88
Old Bull 88
Opequon Creek 18, 56
O'Reilly, John L. 132

P

Paine, Thomas 105, 107
Palatinate, the 29
Pellentz, James 70
Penn, William 38, 99
Phelan, Lawrence 55, 74, 87, 113, 114
Philbrook, Scott 11
Piet, John 111
Piet, Susan 111, 113

poltergeist 14, 17, 50, 51, 52, 54, 69, 81, 83, 104, 108, 119, 125, 127
Pomeroy Foundation 132
Pope John XXII 92
Pope's Night 95
possession 52, 86, 87
Purgatory 23, 24, 47, 52, 81, 86, 88

R

Reformation, the 47, 63, 95, 106
Reign of Terror 106
Reverend Lekeu 60, 113

S

Salem Witch Trials 14, 50, 86, 98, 99, 103
Sánchez, Eduardo 123
Scot, Reginald 95
Shea, John Gilmary 36
Shepherdstown Register 32
Shepherdstown, West Virginia 19
Sherwood, Grace 99
Sinclair, George 115
slavery 27, 39
Smithfield, West Virginia 17, 31, 32, 54, 55, 75, 89
St. John's Point, Ireland 114
St. Louis Leader 60, 109, 110, 111, 113
Stranger, the 20, 32, 34, 36, 37, 55, 80, 88
Streit, Christian 61

T

Taylor, James 32
Taylor, Mary Ann 33, 36, 55
Thirty Years' War 98

V

Virginian 32
Virginia Statute for Religious Freedom 30, 38, 62

Voice, the 23, 46, 72, 73, 75, 79, 81,
    83, 84, 86, 87, 88, 89, 112, 127
Voltaire 42, 99, 107
Von Schmettau, Amalia 41

W

Washington, George 17, 42
Wesley, John 108
Weyer, Johann 95
White, Thomas 68, 91
Willis, James 125
Winchester, Virginia 29, 55, 56, 61,
    65, 88
witchcraft 29, 50, 68, 90, 92, 98, 99,
    104

ABOUT THE AUTHOR

Michael Kishbucher resides in Virginia with his wife and daughters. He first learned intelligence tradecraft while serving in the U.S. Air Force. He earned a Master of Science of Strategic Intelligence degree from the Department of Defense's Joint Military Intelligence College and a Master of Strategy degree from Air War College. He analyzes adversarial military capability for the Defense Intelligence Agency as a civilian in federal service. Michael is getting used to writing in the third person, but it is still weird.